MULTINATIONAL INDUSTRIAL RELATIONS SERIES

No. 4. Latin American Studies
(No. 4e—Colombia)

THE POLITICAL, ECONOMIC, AND LABOR CLIMATE IN COLOMBIA

by

DAVID R. DECKER
Research Specialist
Industrial Research Unit

and

IGNACIO DURAN
Research Assistant
Industrial Research Unit

INDUSTRIAL RESEARCH UNIT
The Wharton School, Vance Hall/CS
University of Pennsylvania
Philadelphia, Pennsylvania 19104
U.S.A.

Library of Congress Catalog Number 82-082996
MANUFACTURED IN THE UNITED STATES OF AMERICA
ISBN: 0-89546-025-4
ISSN: 0149-0818

Foreword

In 1972, the Wharton School's Industrial Research Unit established its Multinational Industrial Relations Research Program to supply:

1. key factual information and research concerning the activities, programs, policies, and potential impact of the international unions—including the "trade secretariats," communist and Christian groups, and the regional European, African, and Asian union blocs;
2. similar information regarding the International Labor Organization, the Organization for Economic Cooperation and Development, the United Nations, the European Community's Economic and Social Committee, and other transnational governmental bodies, which frequently are used for and/or support international union objectives and which have adopted codes of conduct for multinational corporations that could significantly affect international labor relations;
3. evaluation of the political, economic, and labor climate affecting investment return in countries throughout the world;
4. analysis and comparison of employee relations and public policy issues among different countries;
5. special in-depth studies, either as part of the research effort concerned with the above or separately underwritten by special information requests.

The publication of this book, *The Political, Economic, and Labor Climate in Colombia* by Dr. David R. Decker and Ignacio Durán, marks the fifth such study of Latin American countries—those for Mexico, Brazil, Peru, and Venezuela having already been published. In addition, studies have been published for the Philippines, the countries of the Arabian Peninsula, Spain, and India. Studies for the Central American Republics, Argentina, Portugal, Turkey, Greece, Malaysia, and Nigeria are either soon to be published or underway.

Such studies are just one of several research endeavors published pursuant to the Industrial Research Unit's Multinational Industrial Relations Programs. Others include examinations of attempts to expand collective bargaining beyond national boundaries; studies of the history, structure, finances, and policies of international trade union secretariats; comparative studies of employee relations issues in various countries; and analyses of the impact of "guidelines" issued by international governmental agencies. A complete list of Industrial Research Unit publications in these and other areas is found on the back covers.

The authors of this study, David R. Decker and Ignacio Durán, are uniquely qualified for the task. Dr. Decker received his undergraduate degree at Grinnell College, and his M.A. and Ph.D. at the University of Kansas. He taught in the Romance Language departments at the University of Oklahoma, the College of Charleston, and the University of Nebraska. He has published several papers in professional journals, is fluent in Spanish, and is currently serving as Research Specialist in the Industrial Research Unit and working toward his Master of Business Administration degree.

Mr. Ignacio Durán has an undergraduate degree in industrial engineering from the Universidad de Los Andes in his native Bogotá, Colombia, and taught statistics at the Colegio San Carlos there. In 1981, he received both a master's degree in engineering from the University of Pennsylvania College of Engineering and a Master of Business Administration degree from the Wharton School. While at Wharton, he served as a research assistant in the Industrial Research Unit. He is now employed in Mexico City.

Many persons assisted with this work. Initial research was performed by former Industrial Research Unit research assistants, all now working in industry or financial institutions: Ms. Nancy R. Johnson, Ms. Cecilia M. Valente, and Ms. Grace F. Hemphill. It was edited by the Unit's former Chief Editor, Ms. Cheryl DellaPenna, and the index was prepared by Ms. Hondi Duncan Brasco. Mrs. Margaret E. Doyle, Office Manager, handled the various administrative matters involved. The study was financed by contributions of our Multinational Research Advisory Group Information Service subscribers. Such funds are unrestricted, although it is understood that they will be used for multinational industrial relations studies. The authors are, of course, solely responsible for the study's content and for the research and views expressed, which should not be attributed to the University of Pennsylvania or to the Multinational Research Advisory Group.

HERBERT R. NORTHRUP, *Director*
Industrial Research Unit
The Wharton School
University of Pennsylvania

Philadelphia
September 1982

TABLE OF CONTENTS

LIST OF TABLES

TABLE PAGE

LIST OF FIGURES

COLOMBIA

CARIBBEAN SEA
PANAMA
PACIFIC OCEAN
VENEZUELA
ECUADOR
BRAZIL
PERU
Riohacha
Santa Marta
Barranquilla
Atlantico
Cartagena
Sincelejo
Montería
GUAJIRA
MAGDALENA
CESAR
SUCRE
BOLIVAR
CORDOBA
ANTIOQUIA
Norte de Santander
Cucuta
Rio Cauca
Bucaramanga
SANTANDER
ARAUCA
Arauca
Río Meta
Puerto Carreño
Medellin
Quibdó
CALDAS
CUNDINAMARCA
Tunja
Risaralda
CHOCO
Armenia
Bogota
BOYACA
VICHADA
Ibague
Rio Magdalena
Villavicencio
VALLE
TOLIMA
Cali
Rio Guaviare
Obando
META
CAUCA
Neiva
Popayán
GUAINIA
HUILA
VAUPES
NARIÑO
Florencia
Pasto
Mitú
Mocoa
CAQUETA
PUTUMAYO
Rio Caquetá
AMAZONAS
N
W
E
S
Rio Putumayo
Rio Amazonas
Leticia

CHAPTER I

Introduction

Colombia, the fifth largest republic in Latin America, is located in northern South America and has coastlines on both the Caribbean Sea and the Pacific Ocean. The political and economic development of the country has been strongly affected by geographic factors: three arms of the Andes Mountains run roughly north and south through the center of the country, dividing the most fertile and productive areas into three long valleys which contain the majority of the population. This has produced an economy and an urbanization pattern much less centralized than that of many Latin American countries. In contrast to countries like Venezuela and Peru, whose economic infrastructures are dominated by their respective capital cities, Colombia has at least four major economic and population centers far removed from Bogotá. This decentralization is also reflected in the transportation and communication networks, which instead of resembling a single wheel with spokes radiating out from the center are more akin to a series of smaller wheels, each the center of a regional market and each connected to the other centers by major road and rail links.

Colombia was the first South American nation to declare its independence from Spain. After a tumultuous period of political activity, the country emerged as a modern state with the ratification of the Constitution of 1886. Industry began to develop in the 1920s, and growth accelerated after World War II. Today, Colombian industry is the most diversified among the nations of the Andean Group (Colombia, Bolivia, Venezuela, Peru, Ecuador).

The organized labor movement in Colombia, after a long period of slow growth, began to gain real importance in the 1930s and 1940s under the sponsorship of the Liberal Party. The labor movement lost its momentum during the dictatorship of Gustavo Rojas Pinilla (1953-1957), but has since begun to grow again. Today, there are about 1.5 million organized workers in Colombia, grouped into four major confederations and several independent organizations.

This study describes the political, economic, and labor conditions prevailing in Colombia today. The emphasis is on recent events, but historical references are made when they help to shape or explain current concerns. Basic information about Colombia is provided in Table I-1.

TABLE I-1
Colombia at a Glance

Area	440,000 square miles.
Population	27.0 million (1979). 71 percent urban, 29 percent rural. Rate of population increase was 2 percent per year in 1981.
Major Cities	Bogotá, the capital (4,324,000); Medellín (1,589,000); Cali (1,382,000); Barranquilla (891,000).
Political System	Civilian democracy with executive, legislative, and judicial branches. Politics is dominated by two traditional parties, the Liberals and the Conservatives.
Economy	Per capita GDP in 1979 was US$1,100. Average GDP growth between 1975 and 1980 was 5.8 percent. The economy is dominated by agriculture (24 percent), manufacturing (22 percent), and commerce (13 percent).
Trade	Total exports for the year ending October 1, 1981, were US$2.95 billion. Total imports for the same period were US$3.87 billion. Major exports are coffee and other farm products; major imports are oil, machinery, chemicals, and transportation equipment.
Inflation	26.4 percent in 1981.
Labor Force	Economically active population in 1981 was 6.318 million; 33 percent in agriculture, 17 percent in services, and 12 percent in manufacturing.
Labor Unions	Four major national confederations with 1.14 million members; independent unions with 200,000 to 400,000 members.
Official Exchange Rate	US$1=Col. Ps. 60.60 (June 1982).

Wherever possible, footnotes have been provided to substantiate the data presented in this study. Some of the information, however, is the product of conversations with labor specialists, businessmen with experience in Colombia, and Colombian scholars. Regrettably, not all of the latter sources can be duly acknowledged in the text.

CHAPTER II

Politics in Colombia

Between 1948 and 1964, Colombia experienced the most extended and bloody period of civil strife in the modern history of Latin America. Approximately 200,000 Colombians died by violence during this period, which is known as the "violencia." One of the causes of the violence was political conflict between the two dominant political parties in the country, and in an effort to end the strife these two parties formed a "National Front" (Frente Nacional) government in 1958, which lasted until 1978. Both the "violencia" and the National Front arose out of historical factors that require discussion if the contemporary scene is to be understood.

BACKGROUND

Historically, Colombian politics has been dominated by two major parties: the Liberals and the Conservatives. The ideological differences between the two parties date back to the nineteenth century, although at that time neither party had a coherent political program in the modern sense. In general, the Liberals favored free trade, a considerable degree of local autonomy, restrictions on the privileges of the Catholic Church, and abolition of slavery. The Conservatives preferred a strong central government, close links between Church and state, and state intervention in the economy. The Liberal constituency was (and still is) primarily urban, with strong support from the commercial classes, trade unionists, and the blacks who live along the Caribbean coast. The core of Conservative support has traditionally been the deeply religious rural dwellers—often dominated by local bosses exercising hereditary control over small villages—and the landed aristocracy.

In the nineteenth century, the transfer of power from one party to another was frequently accompanied by considerable violence, often on the scale of civil war. A civil war in 1879 caused 80,000 deaths, while violence in the period 1899-1903 led to 100,000 deaths.[1] Although there were significant differences of opinion between Liberals and Conservatives on questions of policy in the late nineteenth century, both parties were basically elitist and served the interests of small groups of people. The existence of a literacy and property requirement in order to be eligible to vote prevented most of the people from participating in politics.

The Conservatives ruled Colombia for the first thirty years of the twentieth century. During this period, the development of commercial coffee-growing produced export income that allowed for the beginnings of industrialization in the Medellín area. The loss of Panama to the United States, although a blow to Colombian pride, led to the payment of considerable compensation to the Colombian government. Much of this money was invested in improving, or in many cases creating, the infrastructure required for economic development: roads, railroads, electric power generation, and communications. Economic growth in the 1920s was impressive, and the expansion had important social effects. The shift from subsistence farming to cash-crop farming made many peasants dependent on national or regional markets for their food supply, and squatters began to occupy unused land owned by absentee landlords. This led to many confrontations between squatters, tenant farmers, landowners, and the police. In addition, labor unions began to flex their muscles, organizing strikes against oil companies and against the American-owned United Fruit Company (since 1970, the United Brands Company).

The Conservative Party's long tenure in power and the economic stresses leading up to the Great Depression caused a serious rift within Conservative ranks. The government had been shaken by the United Fruit Company strike, which had resulted in the death of many strikers, and by rising discontent in the countryside. These factors led to the election of a Liberal to the presidency in 1930, beginning a period of Liberal rule that lasted until 1946. The first years of Liberal rule were relatively uneventful, but with the accession of Alfonso López Pumarejo to the presidency in 1934 a more reformist approach emerged.

---

1 John A. Crow, *The Epic of Latin America* (New York: Doubleday & Co., 1971), p. 619.

López Pumarejo proposed a series of sweeping changes in many areas of national life. He enacted a graduated income tax and an excess profits tax, and led congress to a major constitutional revision that excluded priests from public office, removed public education from the control of the Church, eliminated the property and literacy requirements for voting, provided for the expropriation of private property under certain conditions, and decreed that arable land that went uncultivated for a period of ten consecutive years would revert to state ownership.[2]

Despite the radical nature of these changes, their effect was attenuated by strong opposition from within López Pumarejo's own Liberal Party, as well as from the Conservatives. The wide powers granted to the state by the constitutional codification of 1936 were seldom implemented, and despite the extensive proscription of Church influence the educational system continued to be dominated by Catholicism. López Pumarejo's program failed because it was a conscious attempt to modernize the country, while most of the Liberal leaders were content to enjoy the perquisites of office, from which they had been excluded for thirty years, and were not particularly interested in sweeping social changes. The implementation of López Pumarejo's reform program was further delayed by the election of a moderate Liberal, Eduardo Santos, to the presidency in 1938. Although López Pumarejo was reelected in 1942, by that time the opposition to him both from within Liberal ranks and from the Conservatives was much stronger than it had been during his first administration. A deep split had developed within the Liberal Party over the speed with which reforms should be carried out and over the ultimate objectives of the reforms themselves. The radical and populist faction of the Liberal Party was led by Jorge Eliecer Gaitán, who strongly denounced the moderate program of the Liberal majority. Gaitán was a charismatic figure who attracted a wide following among peasants and urban workers.

López Pumarejo was forced to resign in 1945, and presidential elections were held in 1946. Believing that his popularity among the lower classes would enable him to be elected without the backing of a major party, Gaitán refused to support the official Liberal candidate. The split in Liberal ranks led to the election of the Conservative candidate, Mariano Ospina Perez.

---

[2] Robert H. Dix, *Colombia: The Political Dimensions of Change* (New Haven: Yale University Press, 1967), pp. 86-88.

After the election of Ospina, large segments of the Liberal Party came under the influence of Gaitán, who was able to assume official leadership of the party in 1948. Gaitán had succeeded in arousing the political participation of many previously disenfranchised groups, particularly peasants who had long lived under the domination of local bosses, and between 1946 and 1948 he built a mass movement that seemed destined to oust the Conservatives easily. Gaitán was murdered in Bogotá in April 1948, however, triggering mass riots which resulted in several thousand deaths within a few days. This event is usually regarded as the beginning of thc "violencia."

The "Violencia"

Many theories have been advanced to explain the widespread warfare and banditry in the countryside that followed the murder of Gaitán. There was certainly an element of revenge, at least at first, and also a release of Liberal frustration over the failure of the reform efforts. But much of the violence was also caused by simple banditry, rivalries between small villages, local struggles for power, and partisan hatreds. The Conservative government, under Ospina and later under Laureano Gómez, was unable to quell the disturbances in the countryside, in part because of a split within the army and the police between Conservative and Liberal partisans. Frustration with the government's failures in this and other areas led to a military coup d'état in 1953, through which the commander in chief of the army, Gustavo Rojas Pinilla, became president.

The Rojas Pinilla regime was at first fairly popular, mainly because of its initial success in reducing the scale of rural violence. As time went on, however, Rojas Pinilla began to run into opposition from the traditional parties and lost public favor because of his lack of a clearly defined program. His attempt to establish government-run trade unions and to form a third political party alienated strong traditional interest groups. In addition, the Rojas Pinilla regime was the first military regime in Colombia since the nineteenth century, and two previous peaceful transfers of power from one party to another (in 1930 and in 1946) had perhaps reduced public tolerance for an extended extraconstitutional government.

Whatever the reasons for the government's decline in popularity, by 1957 the army was prepared to act on its own. Rojas Pinilla was deposed by his own subordinates, who formed a provisional government for the purpose of returning the country to civilian rule. The mechanism by which this goal was to be achieved was the National Front, initially a coalition of Liberal and Conservative leaders whose objective was to reduce political strife by essentially eliminating electoral competition for a period of sixteen years.

THE NATIONAL FRONT (1958-1974)

The National Front resulted from a series of agreements, formalized by a referendum held in 1957, by which the presidency of the country would be held first by a Liberal, then by a Conservative, and so on successively until 1974. Representation in congress and other deliberative bodies was to be on an equal basis. In retrospect, this cooperation between the two parties can be seen as eminently in their own interests, if not in the interests of their programs. For many years, the conflicts between Liberals and Conservatives were related less to their programs than to the ambitions of individual leaders and the protection of certain special interests. Both parties saw in the military government of Rojas Pinilla, and in the abortive attempt to establish a third party, a threat to their traditional domination of the country's political life.

Popular support for the National Front was strong at first, based on the belief that most of the violence that still plagued the rural areas was politically motivated and that a truce between the parties would bring peace to the country. The governments of the National Front made little effort to promote economic development in a systematic way, however; thus, economically motivated violence persisted in the countryside well into 1964. In addition, the monopoly on power exercised by the two main parties, and the fact that elections were of little significance (since the outcome was predetermined) led to widespread disaffection with the political system. Although the National Front was fairly successful in suppressing violence between the parties, this was replaced by violence within the parties between supporters and opponents of the National Front idea. Because each party was eventually guaranteed a term in power, internal control of the party out of power became as important as electoral supremacy over the opposition party.

Another major result of the National Front truce between the Liberal and Conservative parties was the growth of minor opposition groups that could not find expression of their views within the framework of the National Front coalition. Many of these groups were regionalist in nature and armed themselves well enough to require the use of the army to bring their areas back under the control of the national government. On a national scale, two dissident movements of considerable importance arose in opposition to the National Front. The first, comprising forces in the Liberal Party that had previously supported Gaitán and López Pumarejo, was the Revolutionary Liberal Movement (Movimiento Revolucionario Liberal—MRL). Led by Alfonso López Michelsen (who later became president), the MRL attracted support from landless peasants, civil servants, the Communist Party, and university students. Its program included agrarian reform and restrictions on foreign control of economic activities. At first, the MRL enjoyed considerable electoral success, but by 1967 López Michelsen had led the movement back into the mainstream of the Liberal Party in an effort to wrest control of that party from its traditional leaders.

The other major opposition group that emerged during the National Front period was the National Popular Alliance (Alianza Nacional Popular—ANAPO), led by former military President Rojas Pinilla. This movement is much more difficult to categorize. Although Rojas Pinilla himself was a Conservative, and although ANAPO drew the vast majority of its supporters from Conservative peasants, its program was quite radical. It attracted support both from the major labor confederations and from the lower ranks of the Catholic clergy, who saw in its steadfast opposition to the National Front a chance to break the traditional hold of the Liberal and Conservative elites over the national political scene. Electorally, ANAPO was more successful than the MRL. By the time of the 1970 presidential elections, Liberal and Conservative leaders feared that Rojas Pinilla's organizational efforts might lead to his election. The official candidate of the National Front, Misael Pastrana, was eventually declared the victor, but only after a long recount carried out under a state of siege. The final results showed Pastrana with 40 percent of the vote, Rojas Pinilla with 38 percent, and two minor candidates with the remainder.[3] This near-defeat of the Front candidate was a clear indication that the truce between Liberals

[3] Jean-Pierre Bernard et al., *Guide to the Political Parties of South America*, trans. Michael Perl (Baltimore: Penguin Books, 1973), p. 328.

and Conservatives was breaking down in anticipation of the return to competitive politics in the municipal elections of 1972.

ANAPO went into decline after 1970, as Rojas Pinilla's age and illness reduced his organizing activity. Rojas Pinilla's daughter was the ANAPO candidate in 1974, but she was soundly defeated by the National Front official candidate, Alfonso López Michelsen. Both parties (Liberal and Conservative) engaged in an abortive attempt to extend the duration of the National Front system until 1982;[4] although this effort failed with respect to the presidential succession, cabinet appointments are still made according to the old National Front formula. López Michelsen's administration (1974-1978), the last of the National Front governments, was fortunate in that rising exports brought the current account into balance and then into surplus, but it was beset by renewed violence in the countryside and by a rapid increase in the drug traffic. López Michelsen won the election on a radical-sounding platform of agrarian reform and affiliation of the Liberal Party to the Socialist International, but once in office his policies were almost indistinguishable from those of Pastrana.

Any fair evaluation of the National Front period must concede that violence was drastically reduced and that a measure of political stability was achieved, although at the cost of widespread voter apathy. The truce between the Liberals and the Conservatives allowed transfers of power from one party to the other to take place peacefully, and the "parity" rule for cabinet appointments and local patronage kept the personal ambitions of individual party leaders from leading to violence. On the other hand, the fact that each party was guaranteed a certain amount of time in power made political leaders even more prone than they had previously been to proposing grandiose economic development plans during election campaigns, while reverting to politics as usual after the elections. In addition, the traditional elitism of the two parties was reinforced by the National Front parity arrangements. In the elections of 1974, for example, every major presidential candidate (including the candidate of the supposedly populist ANAPO) were children of ex-presidents of Colombia.

THE CONTEMPORARY SCENE (1978-1982)

The presidential elections of 1978 were the first freely contested presidential elections since 1949. The Liberals were ex-

---

[4] Reza Rezazadeh and Joseph McKenzie, *Political Parties in Colombia* (Ann Arbor: University Microfilms, 1978), p. 72.

pected to win, and a sharp contest took place for the Liberal nomination. For the first time in Colombian history, a presidential primary was held through which the candidate of the Liberal Party would be chosen by popular vote rather than by decision of the party leadership. Julio César Turbay Ayala won the nomination and went on to defeat Conservative Belisario Betancur Cuartas in the general election, although by a narrow margin. Voter participation was only 38 percent, reflecting the cynicism and disenchantment which the National Front had intensified. The popular vote was 2,226,163 (48.8 percent) for Turbay and 2,137,987 (46.8 percent) for Betancur.[5] The narrow Liberal margin of victory was probably due to the fact that former President Carlos Lleras Restrepo, a major figure in the Liberal leadership, refused to support the official Liberal candidate. In accordance with the 1968 constitutional amendment requiring that the victorious party in presidential elections grant "equitable" representation in the cabinet to the losing party, Turbay appointed several Conservatives to ministerial positions.

Turbay took action early in his administration to suppress the rising guerilla violence, which had spread from the countryside to the cities and which now included kidnapings for ransom and drug-related killings. Late in 1978 a "national security statute" was approved that gave the army responsibility for controlling guerilla and drug activity. Martial law was declared in Guajira province, and the army gained considerable initial success in its antiguerilla campaign. The army's campaign was directed primarily against the Revolutionary Armed Forces of Colombia (Fuerzas Armadas Revolucionarios de Colombia—FARC), the oldest and best-organized guerilla group. This group was largely brought under control, but a newer guerilla organization, called "M-19," grew in strength despite the army's efforts. "M-19" is a heterogeneous group with no clear ideological stance. Apart from kidnapings and raids on isolated police and army posts, the group's major attack was the seizure of the Dominican Embassy in Bogotá in early 1980. Although the crisis was resolved peacefully, with the terrorists flying to Havana and the hostages released, the episode clearly showed how far the government is from controlling guerilla activity.

The guerilla problem is complicated by the existence of a large and powerful criminal underworld connected with the drug trade,

---

[5] "Ruling party's choice apparent victor in Colombia," *The New York Times*, June 6, 1978, p. A3.

and by Cuban involvement in the training and arming of revolutionaries. The occasional cooperation between the guerillas and the drug traffickers arises from a natural confluence of interests: both groups operate underground, and both groups depend on the movement of illegal cargo into and out of the country. In addition, the vast sums of money involved in the drug trade have produced considerable corruption, not only among government officials but also in the lower ranks of the military. This has sapped army morale and hurt the antiguerilla campaign.

Documentary evidence of Cuban involvement in the training of "M-19" guerillas led to the expulsion of all Cuban diplomats from Colombia and the withdrawal of the Colombian representatives in Cuba in mid-1981. Before his departure, the Cuban ambassador attempted to justify the training by stating to the Colombian foreign minister that Cuba is obliged to give its moral support to all leftist guerillas.[6] The revelations led to a considerable shift in Colombian foreign policy toward increased cooperation with neighboring democratic states and opposition to Cuban interventionism.

On the whole, the army's campaign against M-19 has not been very successful. In mid-1981 the guerillas abandoned their urban campaign and shifted their operations to the southeastern jungles. Repeated confrontations between the army and the guerillas in that area have led to the complete censorship of radio broadcasts on the insurgency; army commanders would like to see the censorship extended to newspapers and magazines as well. This indicates that the army fears a concentrated guerilla base of operations, even in an isolated area, more than it did the sporadic urban violence that had been the previous tactic of M-19. Turbay also attempted peaceful solutions to the guerilla conflict; he granted a partial amnesty in 1978, and in 1981 he established a "peace commission" led by former President Lleras Restrepo that is implicitly empowered to negotiate with the guerillas. Guerilla leaders claimed that they would cease fighting if all jailed terrorists were released and if their leader were allowed to run for president.[7] It is unlikely, however, that guerilla activity would decline significantly even if these two conditions were

---

6 "Colombians combat Cuban interference," *The New York Times*, August 13, 1981, p. A3.

7 "Guerillas in Colombia quit cities to open a jungle offensive," *The New York Times*, November 11, 1981, p. A6.

met, since the M-19 leadership is divided into many different camps.

On the economic front, Turbay's main effort was a five-year development plan called the National Integration Plan, which is described below in Chapter III. This plan is unusual in Colombian history not for its ambitious scope (many ambitious plans have been proposed by other presidents) but because some of its goals have actually been achieved. A 1981 government report evaluating the first two years of the plan's operation indicated that 83 percent of the total investment program was actually implemented. The completion rate in certain key sectors was even higher: social programs at 95 percent of target, urban and regional development programs at 90 percent of target, and agriculture at 83 percent of target.[8] These are impressive figures for a country in which economic development plans have traditionally been regarded as essentially rhetorical devices useful only during election campaigns.

Electoral participation in the presidential elections of May 1982 was higher than in most recent elections. Out of a total of about 13 million registered voters, more than 7 million Colombians voted, or about 54 percent of the total electorate. The Liberal Party was weakened by a split between López Michelsen, the party's official candidate, and a splinter group called "New Liberalism," led by Luis Carlos Galan. Galan had the support of former President Lleras Restrepo. The Conservatives were united behind Belisario Betancur, who had run for president unsuccessfully in 1978. A small leftist coalition comprising communists and socialists put forward Gerardo Molina as its candidate.

The split in Liberal ranks enabled Betancur to win the election by a comfortable margin of about 400,000 votes over López Michelsen. Betancur polled about 47 percent of the vote, against slightly more than 40 percent for López Michelsen and almost 12 percent for Galan. The leftist coalition won about 1 percent of the vote.[9] Despite the fact that congressional elections held earlier in 1982 had been marred by M-19-sponsored violence, the presidential elections were comparatively peaceful and orderly.

Betancur had run on a probusiness platform, calling for tax incentives for industrial development, eased credit for domestic expansion, export credits, and renewed emphasis on agricultural

---

[8] "Colombia Claims High Completion Rate for Development Plan," *Business Latin America*, August 19, 1981, pp. 258-259.

[9] "Conservative wins in Colombia," *The New York Times*, June 1, 1982, p. A4.

production. He may encounter problems in congress, which is still controlled by the Liberal Party, but the size of his plurality and the increasingly conservative political mood of the country should help him carry out a considerable part of his program.

See Table II-1 for a profile of the political organization of contemporary Colombia.

TABLE II-1

A Profile of Colombia's Political Organization

Administration	A democratic state with power relatively centralized in the national government. The country is divided into twenty-two states ("departamentos") and eight territories (four "intendencias" and four "comisarias"). The territories lack local legislatures. Bogotá is governed separately as a Federal District. Colombia has been under civilian rule since 1958, although a state of siege declared during the 1950s is still in effect and the military has fairly wide powers.
Parties	Colombian politics has traditionally been dominated by the two major parties, the Liberals and the Conservatives. Between 1958 and 1974, these two parties alternated in power according to a coalition plan known as the "National Front." Since 1978, elections are fully free and the winning party is not required to appoint members of the losing party to cabinet posts, although this is frequently done as a conciliatory gesture. Party affiliation is often determined by tradition rather than by ideology, particularly in rural areas. Both parties contain diverse ideological tendencies.
Executive	The president is the chief executive officer and wields powers considerably broader than those of the U.S. president, including the right to appoint state governors without the consent of congress. The president appoints all cabinet ministers and heads of administrative departments. Presidential decisions affecting the area of responsibility of cabinet ministers must be countersigned by the responsible cabinet minister. Under the state of siege, the president is empowered to request special authority which, if judged constitutional by the Supreme Court of Justice, becomes effective immediately.
Legislative	Congress is divided into a Senate, consisting of 113 senators, and a House of Representatives, consisting of 199 members. The number of senators and representatives and the composition of their districts are adjusted after each national census. The power of congress is more limited than in many democratic countries; congress may originate legislation in many areas but the crucial budgetary and economic planning functions remain with the executive branch.

TABLE II-1 (continued)

Judicial	Justice is administered by a twenty-member Supreme Court of Justice, superior district tribunals, superior courts, circuit courts, courts of criminal instruction, and municipal courts. Labor matters are heard in a system of regional labor courts and in the Division of Labor Cassation of the Supreme Court of Justice. In addition to the system of criminal and civil courts, there is a parallel system of administrative tribunals which rule on administrative disputes.

Source: Pan American Union, *A Statement of the Laws of Colombia in Matters Affecting Business*, 4th ed., Supplement No. 2 (Washington, D.C.: Pan American Union, 1969).

POLITICAL OUTLOOK

Colombia's political future will depend on the extent to which the major parties succeed in responding to popular pressures for social and economic change. The National Front period allowed the two major parties to entrench themselves firmly in the government bureaucracy, and the lack of clear ideological differences between the two parties has created a deep cynicism in the Colombian electorate. Turbay's efforts to follow through on his economic plan may have restored some confidence in the government, but a real reform of both parties (internal reform as well as clarification of ideological stance) will be necessary if public confidence and participation in politics is to increase.

Apart from electoral apathy, other major problems persist. The National Integration Plan has not stimulated economic growth to the extent that the government had hoped, and large amounts of capital remain outside the legal capital markets because of the drug trade. The drug trade has also had a debilitating effect on the general level of public morality and has reinforced the public impression that many government officials are extremely corrupt. The guerilla movement has no real chance of toppling the government, but its activities are a constant reminder to the public that the country is not really at peace. Neither the Liberal Party nor the Conservative Party has been successful in attracting the support of the large numbers of disaffected urban workers and rural dwellers. Colombia continues to be governed by an elite whose interests, despite their affiliation to different political parties, are very similar. While this arrangement brings stability in the short run, it is likely to produce an increasing informal opposition in the future.

CHAPTER III

The Colombian Economy in Profile

Two major factors distinguish the Colombian economy of the 1980s from the one existing twenty years ago. The rate of population growth has declined from 3.2 percent in 1964 to about 2 percent in 1982. This decline has had a profound effect on the composition and size of the labor force. The other major change is in the healthy level of international reserves, which indicates that the external sector is no longer the economic bottleneck it was in the 1960s.

During his presidency, Turbay Ayala launched a development plan, called the National Integration Plan (Plan de Integración Nacional—PIN), aimed at overcoming the effects of the excessive fiscal restraint of the previous government and achieving stable growth. The objective of the development plan is to expand the national market and integrate the different regions of the country by improving the transportation and communications infrastructure. Inflation, the erosion of real income, excessive indebtedness, and high interest rates are the greatest problems in the short run.

INFRASTRUCTURE

Transportation, communications, and energy are discussed in this section.

Transportation and Ports

Historically, the development of transportation in Colombia has lagged behind other sectors of the economy because of the immense practical difficulties caused by rugged mountainous terrain. The vast majority of the Colombian population lives in three large valleys separated by imposing mountain ranges. Tables III-1 and III-2 present a breakdown of the relative importance of road, rail, river, and air transportation in the movement of cargo and passengers.

TABLE III-1
Transportation System Distribution
(Cargo)

	National (million tons/kilometer)						International (thousand tons)		
Year	Roads [a]	Railroad	River	Pilotage	Air	Subtotal	Ports [b]	Air	Subtotal
1970	9,318	1,173	1,545	786	85	12,907	2,599	19.5	2,618.5
1971	9,997	1,150	1,319	843	79	13,388	2,709	25.0	2,734.0
1972	10,501	1,198	1,451	2,116	121	15,387	2,652	28.0	2,680.0
1973	11,433	1,331	2,003	2,482	124	17,374	3,068	30.7	3,098.7
1974	12,346	1,329	2,585	3,240	152	19,652	3,227	45.8	3,272.8
1975	13,958	1,139	2,400	2,398	144	20,039	2,864	48.2	2,912.2
1976	14,461	1,159	1,609	2,535	138	19,902	2,696	50.8	2,746.8
1977	17,025	1,207	1,820	2,650	146 [c]	22,848	3,500	71.1	3,571.1
1978	18,286 [c]	1,158 [c]	1,800 [c]	2,780 [c]	155 [c]	24,179 [c]	3,808	n.a.	—

Source: Departamento Nacional de Planeación, *Plan de Integración Nacional,* Vol. II (Bogotá: Biblioteca del Desarrollo—DNP, 1980), p. 142.

[a] Includes urban transportation.
[b] Does not include cargo loaded in private docks.
[c] Estimate.
n.a. = not available.

TABLE III-2
Transportation System Distribution
(Passengers)

	National					International (thousands of passengers)
Year	Roads[a]	Railroads	River	Air	Subtotal	
1970	41,115	249	1	2,067	43,432	467
1971	44,292	281	7	1,953	46,533	524
1972	47,356	398	4	2,273	50,031	596
1973	51,586	427	4	2,539	54,556	685
1974	55,683	482	4	2,702	58,871	815
1975	60,042	523	4	2,870	63,439	891
1976	66,109	511	5	3,226	69,851	966
1977	71,175	392	4	3,664[b]	75,235	1,041
1978	75,771[b]	348	4	4,213[b]	80,336[b]	1,140[b]

Source: DNP, *Plan de Integración Nacional,* Vol. II, p. 142.
[a] Includes urban transportation.
[b] Estimate.

Colombia's road network is divided for administrative purposes into three systems: the national trunk highway system, the regional road system, and local secondary roads. Together, the three systems comprise about 72,000 kilometers, of which only 12 percent are paved. The national roads are built and maintained by the Ministry of Public Works and Transportation, the regional roads are the responsibility of the individual states, and the secondary roads are funded through the National Fund for Secondary Roads (Fondo Nacional de Caminos Vecinales). Financing for all three types of road ultimately comes from taxes on gasoline and diesel fuel, as well as tolls and direct budget allocations.[1]

The system of major highways consists of the Western Trunk Highway, running from the Ecuadorean border to the Caribbean coast and passing through Medellín; the Central Trunk Highway, which also starts at the Ecuadorean border and which passes through Bogotá and Bucaramanga before reaching the Caribbean coast; and the Caribbean Trunk Highway, which links the cities on the north coast and leads into Venezuela.

The Colombian road network suffers from poor maintenance and lack of integration. The National Integration Plan calls for

[1] "Road Network Leads in Transportation," *Colombia Today,* Vol. 10, No. 2 (1975), p. 2.

large investments in upgrading existing roads and extending the system; under the first two years of the National Integration Plan, US$712 million was allocated for improving the transportation system. Of this total, only US$557 million, or 78 percent, was actually spent, but this represents a significant increase over previous investments in the transportation infrastructure.[2] Together with the general revamping and extension of the road network, the government also hopes to complete the remaining gaps in the Pan American Highway by 1983.

The railroad network is built around the line running from Bogotá to Santa Marta and its trunk lines to Medellín and Bucaramanga. A line joining the port of Buenaventura in the Pacific and Cali also carries heavy traffic. Roughly 70 percent of the cargo moved by the railway system is transported on these lines.[3] Only 85 percent of the tracks are presently usable and just 38 percent of the rolling stock is operational. The government plans to rehabilitate the whole system by investing US$153 million in modernizing the equipment and repair shops, as well as in improving and expanding the existing tracks.[4]

Four systems make up the 8,399 kilometers of navigable rivers in Colombia: the Amazon (south), Orinoco (east), Atrato-San Juan (west), and the Magdalena system. The latter is by far the most important, with about 98 percent of the total traffic. River transportation is suitable for oil derivatives, cement, coal, and fertilizers and is currently being used intensively for these products between Barrancabermeja (an oil center) and the ports of Barranquilla (on the Magdalena estuary) and Cartagena (through the man-made Canal del Dique).

Three ports on the Atlantic (Barranquilla, Cartagena, and Santa Marta) and two on the Pacific (Buenaventura and Tumaco) provide the infrastructure for most of the maritime trade of Colombia. US$90 million has been earmarked to improve the equipment and service standards of the ports to accommodate Colombia's increasing foreign trade.[5]

---

[2] "Colombia Claims High Completion Rate for Development Plan," *Business Latin America*, August 19, 1981, p. 259.

[3] Departamento Nacional de Planeación (DNP), *Plan de Integración Nacional*, Vol. II (Bogotá: Biblioteca del Desarrollo—DNP, 1980), p. 160.

[4] "Colombia's Transportation System," *Colombia Today*, Vol. 14, No. 8 (1979), pp. 2-3.

[5] *Ibid.*, p. 3.

Given the difficulties posed by the Andes, air transportation is the only way to integrate many areas with the rest of the country, and its importance will increase in the 1980s. All of the state and territorial capitals have airports, but only 15 can accommodate jets. Regional and military airports complete the network of 667 registered airports.[6] The facilities in Bogotá, Barranquilla, Medellín, and Cartagena need modernizing in order to meet current demand; work in Bogotá and Medellín has already begun. Navigational aid services also need improvement. Colombia is served by eleven international passenger airlines and ten national companies. Avianca is the largest and best known of the Colombian airlines.

Communications

Colombia's telecommunications network is made up of local networks, usually administered by municipal companies, and the federally operated, long-distance system. By 1978, the number of telephones per 100 residents was 4.8. Service has expanded at an average annual rate of 8.5 percent during the past twenty years. In the last ten years the government has attempted to improve the integration of the local and long-distance systems by concentrating on the installation of linking circuits. About 5,000 communities (mostly smaller than 2,500 inhabitants) still lack telephone service.

There are 1,626 telegraph offices in the country, 41 telex stations, 230 offices linked to the gentex network, and 3,560 subscribers to gentex and telex. Inravisión (Instituto Nacional de Radio y Televisión) is the state enterprise responsible for administering the television network in Colombia. The largest commercial network reaches 85 percent of the population, while the smaller one reaches 44 percent. The national post office (Adpostal) handles the collection and delivery of mail in Colombia. Air mail service is provided by Avianca under contract to Adpostal.

Oil, Natural Gas, and Coal

Like most oil-importing nations, Colombia is attempting to diversify its sources of energy to become less dependent on expensive oil imports. Table III-3 shows the breakdown of energy consumption and reserves in 1978. Proved reserves were con-

[6] DNP, *Plan de Integración Nacional*, Vol. II, p. 168.

TABLE III-3

Energy Supply and Proven Reserves, 1978

Source	Energy Supplied (%)	Reserves (petroleum equivalent tons, %)
Oil	51.5	1.3
Natural Gas	19.8	3.9
Coal	21.9	39.5
Hydroelectric	6.8	55.3

Source: DNP, *Plan de Integración Nacional*, Vol. I, p. 113.

verted to equivalent oil tons for purposes of comparison. In the 1980s, Colombia will attempt to shift to its abundant coal and hydroelectric resources. Oil exploration will be intensified, but the emphasis will probably be on increased use of coal, natural gas, and hydroelectric power.

Ecopetrol (Empresa Colombiana de Petróleos) is the state-owned company responsible for administering oil exploration and production policies. It controls and operates the major fields and refineries and supervises the multinational companies that are active in the country. Since 1976, the government has gradually raised the price of gasoline to reduce the amount of subsidies paid by Ecopetrol, which had maintained an unreasonably low gasoline price. Despite these efforts, Ecopetrol occupies an extremely weak financial position, which could jeopardize future development and cause serious monetary and foreign exchange problems if the deficit is financed externally.[7]

Ecopetrol's major operations are located in the mid-Magdalena valley near Bucaramanga, in the oil town of Barrancabermeja. This region contains an important portion of the proved oil reserves. Other fields have been found to the north of Barrancabermeja near the Venezuelan border. Minor discoveries have also been made to the southwest of Bogotá in Huila and Putumayo. More recently, discoveries have been made in the eastern plains (Llanos Orientales) and Antioquía. Recent discoveries may not boost the supply enough to compensate for increased domestic demand, however. Gasoline consumption rose by an average 5.7 percent per year between 1970 and 1978; during that period, oil production declined by an average 6.8 percent.[8] Oil production in

[7] Miguel Urrutia and Ricardo Villaveces, "Perspecivas Energéticas," *La Economía Colombiana en la Década de los Ochenta* (Bogotá: Editorial Presencia, 1979), p. 232.

[8] DNP, *Plan de Integración Nacional*, Vol. II, p. 81.

Colombia declined from a peak of 219,350 barrels per day (bpd) in 1970 to about 146,000 bpd in 1981.[9] Table III-4 illustrates the sharp decline in oil production and the corresponding increase in oil imports.

TABLE III-4
Production and Imports of Crude Oil
(millions of barrels)

Year	Production	Imports	Cost of Imports (millions of US$)
1970	79.6	0	0
1971	78.6	0	0
1972	71.6	0	0
1973	67.0	0	0
1974	61.3	0	0
1975	57.2	0	0
1976	53.3	6.7	83.5
1977	50.1	9.3	130.4
1978	47.7	8.8	119.4
1979	45.3	8.9	297.3
1980	45.9	n.a.	269.0
1981	48.9	n.a.	233.0[a]

Sources: DNP, *Plan de Integración Nacional,* Vol. II, p. 83; *Bank of London and South America Review,* Vol. 15, No. IV/81, pp. 214, 241.
[a] Estimate.
n.a. = not available.

Prior to 1979, the refinery at Barrancabermeja, Colombia's largest, had a capacity of 110,000 bpd. In late 1979, an additional 30,000 bpd capacity was added after a new unit for refining heavy oils began production.[10] The other major refinery is located at Mamonal, near Cartagena. Its output is 50,000 bpd, and planned expansions would increase this figure to 70,000 bpd by 1982.[11] With these expansions, Colombia's refining capacity would reach 225,600 bpd after the output of other minor refineries is included.

The ratio of proved reserves to volume of production dropped from 127 in 1926 to 7.3 in 1979. Current proved reserves are

[9] "Colombia," *Bank of London and South America Review,* Vol. 16, No. I/82, p. 33; "Colombia's Energy Outlook for the 1980's," *Colombia Today,* Vol. 14, No. 12.

[10] Luís Carlos Galán, "La Unidad Balance: Una Obra que Transforma a Ecopetrol," *Nueva Frontera,* December 10-16, 1979, pp. 11-12.

[11] DNP, *Plan de Integración Nacional,* Vol. II, p. 104.

330 million barrels, of which 36 percent is owned by Ecopetrol.[12] Because of the relative stagnation of domestic production, the government has placed high priority on the search for new reserves. The López Michelsen government announced a plan to drill 730 exploratory wells, which will cost US$3-4 billion over a period of ten years. This ambitious plan is faltering, however; between 1976 and 1980, only 23 wells were drilled per year, casting serious doubts on the success of the whole program.[13] Recent developments are more encouraging: the Gulf Oil Corporation, Texas Petroleum, and Exxon Corporation are active in exploration, and important discoveries were made in 1981. In addition, the rate of increase of domestic gasoline declined in 1981 to 1.5 percent after an average annual increase of 7 percent per year in the 1970s.[14]

Current reserves of natural gas are 4,716 trillion cubic feet, equivalent to 926 million barrels of oil.[15] About 73 percent of this total is found in the northern Guajira Peninsula, on the border with Venezuela. A pipeline connecting these deposits with Cartagena facilitates the substitution of gas for petroleum in industrial and electricity-generating plants.[16] Production of natural gas increased by an average of 8.4 percent per year between 1971 and 1978. By 1981, production had reached the equivalent of 75,200 barrels of fuel oil per year.[17] Natural gas is the primary energy source for the Atlantic region, which increased its consumption from 42 percent of the national total in 1970 to 67 percent in 1978. A Japanese firm is studying the possibility of using Colombian natural gas in the production of ammonia and urea. The amount of gas available for such projects and for export (in liquefied form) will probably increase when the government's large coal projects come on stream and coal begins to replace gas as a source of power in electricity-generating plants. The prospects for gas-based projects in Colombia are therefore encouraging.

---

[12] *Ibid.*, p. 84.

[13] "Colombia's Energy Outlook Is Bolstered by Diverse Power Sources," *Business Latin America*, June 11, 1980, p. 189.

[14] "Colombia," *Bank of London and South America Review*, Vol. 16, No. I/82, p. 33.

[15] DNP, *Plan de Integración Nacional*, Vol. II, p. 27.

[16] "Natural Gas Pipeline Expanded," *Colombia Today*, Vol. 12, No. 9 (1979).

[17] "Projections for 1982," *ibid.*, Vol. 16, No. 11 (1981).

Proved reserves of coal are 1.3 billion tons. Total production in 1979 was about 5 million tons, of which 90 percent was consumed locally and 10 percent exported. Until very recently, the coal industry in Colombia was dominated by very small producers: of the 700 mines in operation, about 60 percent produce less than 500 tons per month.

The character and volume of coal mining will change in the early 1980s with the implementation of the Cerrejón project, a very large coal project involving considerable investment in infrastructure as well as in mining. The project originated in 1976 when an agreement was reached between the state-owned Carbones de Colombia (Carbocol) and the International Colombia Resources Corporation, a fully owned susidiary of the Exxon Corporation. The feasibility studies were completed by 1980, and in early 1981 Morris-Knudsen, a U.S. firm, won the US$1.7 billion four-year contract for the development of El Cerrejón.[18] The production target for 1982 is 300,000-400,000 tons, rising to 5 million tons per year by 1985. The coal will be used to fuel two coal-fired power plants and will later replace natural gas in existing plants. The Cerrejón project includes rail and port links, including the construction of a port at Bahía del Portete.[19] Exports of El Cerrejón coal (at production levels of 5 million tons per year) would earn US$600 million per year in foreign exchange.[20]

Carbocol is developing a small mine of its own south of the Cerrejón project. The output from this mine will be used to replace natural gas currently being burned for power generation in plants along the Atlantic Coast. Production is slated to begin in 1982 at 300,000 tons and to rise to 1.5 million tons per year by 1984.[21]

Electricity

Practically all power-generating plants, transmission lines, and distribution networks are state-owned. Bogotá, Cali, Medellín, and the Caribbean coast are served by major public utility corporations: the Bogotá Electric Power Company, the Medellín

---

18 "Colombia," *Bank of London and South America Review*, Vol. 15, No. II/81, p. 93.

19 "Colombia: Summary of the Current Situation," *ibid.*, p. 25.

20 "Colombia's Energy Outlook."

21 DNP, *Plan de Integración Nacional*, Vol. II, p. 123.

Public Utilities Company, the Cauca Valley Corporation, and the Caribbean Regional Electrical Power Institute. The Colombian Institute of Electric Energy is the state organization that supplies small and medium-sized towns not serviced by the major systems. Until 1967 these organizations functioned independently, creating power imbalances in different regions of the country.

To correct this situation, the Electric Interconnection Corporation (ISA) was formed in 1967. With the large existing utility companies as major shareholders, ISA's transmission lines have linked many of Colombia's regional systems since 1972.[22] The three largest cities now operate on a single grid. By 1982, the Caribbean Regional Electrical Power Institute will be integrated into the system. Total installed capacity by year-end 1981 was 4,403 megawatts, of which 72 percent was hydroelectric and 28 percent was thermoelectric. The hydroelectric potential of Colombia is estimated at 93,085 megawatts distributed in 308 projects. Only 22 are presently in operation, with a total capacity of 2,920 megawatts. The thermoelectric system has 16 plants with a combined capacity of 1,116 megawatts.[23]

Most of Colombia's hydroelectric potential (70 percent) lies in the Andes highlands, where approximately 84 percent of the population lives. This favorable condition should ease some of the problems of expanding hydroelectric output. Several hydroelectric projects, with a combined capacity of 2,739 megawatts, are scheduled for completion in 1983, against projections of an average yearly increase in demand of 10 percent.[24]

Bogotá experienced power cuts for three hours daily during most of 1981. The shortages were due to delays in the completion of the Chingaza pipeline projects, delays in the installation of transmission lines linking the capital with the Atlantic coast, and misjudgment on the part of the government which led to a slowdown of work on the new Termozipa V power station. Power rationing ended in late 1981.[25]

The government's development plan called for an investment of US$1,190 million in electricity projects in 1979 and 1980.

---

22 "Colombia Expands Electrical Output," *Colombia Today*, Vol. 10, No. 4 (1975).

23 DNP, *Plan de Integración Nacional*, Vol. II, pp. 55-57.

24 "Colombia's Energy Outlook."

25 "1981 Performance by Sector," *Colombia Today*, Vol. 16, No. 11 (1981).

Government statistics indicate that, of this total proposed investment, US$840 million (71 percent) was actually invested.[26]

ECONOMIC GROWTH

The Colombian economy grew at an average annual rate of 6.1 percent in real terms during the 1970s. Per capita income also increased in real terms during the 1970s, but at a slower rate than the overall economy. Table III-5 presents growth figures for both the overall economy and for per capita income, while Figure III-1 illustrates the increasing gap between the real growth of the economy and the real increase in per capita income.

TABLE III-5
Real Growth in Gross Domestic Product and Per Capita Income

Year	Real GDP Growth (%)	Real Per Capita Income Growth (%)
1970	6.6	3.6
1971	5.8	2.4
1972	7.9	4.5
1973	7.6	5.3
1974	6.5	4.1
1975	4.3	1.9
1976	4.2	1.7
1977	4.7	2.2
1978	8.8	6.2
1979	5.3	2.7
1980	4.0	n.a.
1981	2.5	n.a.

Sources: James W. Wilkie, ed., *Statistical Abstract of Latin America*, Vol. 21 (Los Angeles: UCLA Latin American Center Publications, 1981), p. 279; *Bank of London and South America Review*, Vol. 16, No. I/82, p. 23; *Colombia Today*, Vol. 17, No. 1 (1982).
n.a. = not available.

GDP by Sector

The Colombian economy is still dominated by agriculture, although the percentage of GDP contributed by the agricultural sector has been declining. The manufacturing sector grew at a faster rate than total GDP in the 1970s. Mining has been a small factor in total GDP, although large new projects should

[26] "Colombia Claims High Completion Rate," p. 259.

FIGURE III-1
National Income and Per Capita Income
(1974 = 100)

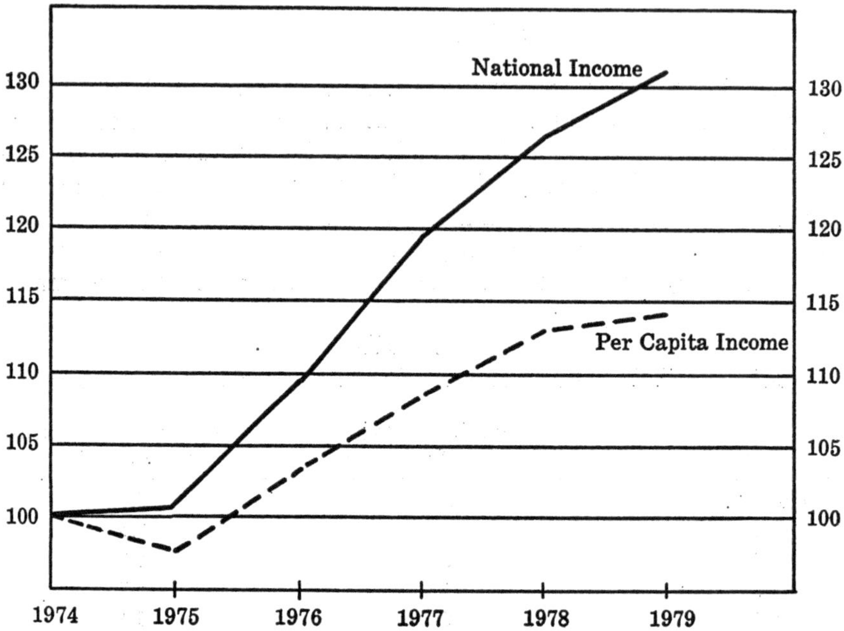

Source: "Colombia—Statistical Survey of the Domestic Economy," *Colombia Today*, Vol. 16, No. 6 (1981).

boost the contribution of this sector in the 1980s. The construction sector, the activity of which peaked during the Pastrana administration because of a development strategy especially tailored to it, has recently performed erratically because of chronic credit shortages. The service sector has gradually expanded its participation to slightly less than 15 percent. Table III-6 presents a breakdown of the Colombian economy by sector, showing the percentages contributed by each sector to total GDP.

Inflation and Monetary Policy

Inflation in the 1970s averaged over 10 percent per year. Variations in the consumer price index (CPI) are given in Table III-7. Despite the government's efforts to keep inflation under control, it reached 26.5 percent in 1980 and was 26.4 percent by year-end 1981, boosted by higher wages, steeper fuel and electricity bills, and increased government spending.[27] Housing costs

[27] "1981 Performance by Sector."

remained under the overall inflation rate due to rent controls imposed by the López Michelsen government, which were recently slackened by the Turbay government. Housing, therefore, can be expected to push inflation up.

Colombia's financial system has operated under a high degree of regulation for the past two decades, which has hampered its effectiveness in mobilizing private savings and allocating resources

TABLE III-6
Gross Domestic Product by Sector
(%)

Sector	1970	1975	1980
Agriculture	27.5	25.9	23.9
Manufacturing	17.5	18.4	22.1
Retail Trade	13.7	13.2	n.a.
Personal Services	7.6	7.6	6.1
Government Services	6.9	6.8	6.1
Transportation and Communications	7.4	8.6	5.5[a]
Construction	5.5	4.8	4.6
Mining	2.1	1.4	1.7
Gas, Electricity, Water	1.5	1.7	1.3
Finance, Insurance	3.6	4.9	n.a.

Sources: For 1970 and 1975, "Qué son y como funcionan los indicadores económicos," *Documentos Nueva Frontera*, No. 49, August 1980, p. 20; for 1980, *Bank of London and South America Review*, Vol. 15, No. IV/81, p. 211.

[a] Transportation only.

n.a. = not available.

TABLE III-7
Increases in the Consumer Price Index
(%)

Year	Total CPI	Food	Housing	Clothing
1977	29.4	34.8	0[a]	22.5
1978	17.8	11.9	50.6	27.5
1979	29.8	32.1	27.5	25.5
1980	26.5	25.4	31.7	22.7
1981	26.4	n.a.	n.a.	n.a.

Sources: Calculated from figures given in: "Colombia—A Statistical Survey of the Domestic Economy," *Colombia Today*, Vol. 16, No. 6 (1981); "1981 Performance by Sector," *Colombia Today*, Vol. 16, No. 11 (1981); *Bank of London and South America Review*, Vol. 16, No. I/82, p. 31.

[a] Rent control was in effect in 1977.

efficiently. There are two tools used by Colombian authorities to fulfill the goals of control and resource allocation in formulating monetary policy. First, reserve requirements are used to control secondary expansion. Second, by monitoring the Central Bank's lending to other banks through the discount window, the government is able to direct credit to specific sectors of the economy, thus fulfilling the goal of resource allocation.

During the early 1970s, Colombia began to enjoy a favorable balance in its reserve account that led monetary authorities to restrain credit. Subsidized credit continued for specific sectors despite increased, but unsatisfied, credit demand. The financial reform of 1974 was intended to eliminate that disparity. The measures taken to tackle the problem were aimed at dismantling the subsidized funds system and allowing the market to allocate funds efficiently. Additionally, open-market operations similar to Treasury Bill auctions in the United States were introduced to control the money supply.

During the second half of the 1970s, the unusual accumulation of international reserves forced monetary authorities to revise their policy. Between 1975 and 1976, international reserves more than doubled, and their growth since then has been significant (see Table III-8). The pressure on the money supply has been tremendous, but it seems to be slowing down (growth in 1980 was the smallest since 1975).

Monetary authorities in Colombia face a no-win situation. Controlling monetary growth necessitates getting involved in open-market operations. To be able to attract investors, government securities (Títulos de Participación) have to offer desirable yields. By raising yields, the government is indirectly raising interest rates. Higher interest rates hamper investment and attract foreign speculative capital, both of which run against government goals. If the government does not intervene, rampant inflation will continue. Monetary authorities, and the government for that matter, will be judged on how well they can balance these conflicting goals.

MAJOR SECTORS OF THE ECONOMY

Despite the difficulties these two sectors have encountered in recent years, agriculture and manufacturing are the backbone of the Colombian economy. Manufacturing has been hurt by low investment and obsolete plants and equipment, while agriculture suffers from the neglect of the central government.

TABLE III-8
International Reserves
(US$ millions)

Year	Reserves	Percent Change over Previous Year
1971	203	n.a.
1972	325	60
1973	534	64
1974	449	—16
1975	521	16
1976	1,158	122
1977	1,820	57
1978	2,503	38
1979	4,058	62
1980	5,033	24
1981	5,630	11

Sources: International Monetary Fund, *International Financial Statistics* (Washington, D.C.: IMF, May 1978), p. 119; *Bank of London and South America Review*, Vol. 15, No. IV/81, p. 241; *Colombia Today*, Vol. 17, No. 1 (1982).
n.a. = not available.

Agriculture

Agriculture's share of the GDP declined from 34 percent in 1960 to 24 percent in 1980. During this same period, employment in agriculture declined from 52 percent of the labor force to 33 percent, reflecting increased mechanization and higher productivity.[28] Agricultural products generated about two-thirds of Colombia's US$2.6 billion total exports in 1981, with coffee remaining the country's principal export commodity. In view of this, it is not surprising that many complaints have been raised against the government's relative lack of interest in the agricultural sector. While agriculture received 26.6 percent of available private credit in 1970, its percentage had dropped to 21.8 percent by 1979. Government investment followed a similar trend. In 1970, 6 percent of all public investment went to agriculture; by 1979 this figure had declined to 2 percent.

Higher costs for agricultural inputs, especially fertilizer, and an overvalued peso are the main restraints on increasing agricul-

[28] *World Development Report, 1980* (Washington, D.C.: International Bank for Reconstruction and Development, 1980), pp. 114, 116.

tural exports. Fertilizer costs in 1980 increased by over 100 percent, while rural wages rose by 20 to 25 percent.[29] Levels of production remain extremely sensitive to international commodity prices and to weather conditions. (Crop output in recent years is summarized in Table III-9.)

TABLE III-9

Trends in Agricultural Production

	Production (in thousands of metric tons)			
Crop	**1979**	**1980**	**1981[a]**	**1982[b]**
Rice	1,932	1,718	1,799	1,867
Potatoes	1,966	1,727	2,100	2,100
Cassava	1,909	2,105	n.a.	n.a.
Sugar	1,096	1,148	1,300	1,250
Corn	870	853	880	850
Coffee	756	762	840	840
Sorghum	501	430	532	550
Cotton	153	186	366	270
Soybeans	146	155	89	100
Barley	137	110	56	60
Beans	75	82	87	89
Wheat	42	46	51	60

Sources: *Agricultural Situation: Western Hemisphere, Review of 1980 and Outlook for 1981* (Washington, D.C.: U.S. Department of Agriculture, Economics and Statistics Service, 1981), pp. 38-41; "Colombian Agriculture: The Outlook Is Not Problem-free," *Business Latin America*, March 24, 1982, p. 95.

[a] Estimates.

[b] Projection.

Coffee production continued its upward trend in the late 1970s, stimulated by higher international prices and the introduction of the new higher-yielding "caturra" variety, now planted in about 25 percent of the total coffee acreage.[30] Production in 1981 reached 12.4 million 60-kilo bags, down slightly from 1980 but

[29] *Agricultural Situation: Western Hemisphere, Review of 1980 and Outlook for 1981* (Washington, D.C.: U.S. Department of Agriculture, Economics and Statistics Service, 1981), p. 26.

[30] "Record coffee exports but the price dips," *Financial Times*, October 6, 1980, p. 23.

still a near-record figure.[31] Production has increased steadily since the 1975 frosts in Brazil, when international prices increased rapidly in response to the destruction of most of Brazil's crop. Production in 1975 was around 8 million bags.[32]

The size of cattle herds increased in 1980 in response to stronger domestic demand and expanded exports to the Soviet Union, Israel, and Peru. The total cattle population in 1980 was 28.4 million head, up 4 percent from 1979. Poultry, meat, and pork production also showed significant increases.

Grains are the principal Colombian agricultural import. Major imports in 1980 were sorghum, 200,000 tons for the feed industry; corn, 130,000 tons for the food industry and as a substitute for sorghum in the feed sector; barley, 70,000 tons for the rapidly expanding brewery industry; and soybean oil, 70,000 tons to meet the growing domestic demand for vegetable oil. Wheat continues to be the major agricultural import, however, with 649,000 tons imported in 1980. Powdered milk, fish oil, tallow, lard, and cacao are other significant imports.[33]

In general, agricultural productivity in Colombia is fairly low. The country's crop output per hectare trails by 2.3 times the average output of the most productive countries for each kind of crop.[34] The government's efforts to improve agricultural productivity have not been vigorous. In the late 1960s, the Lleras Restrepo government introduced an agrarian reform program aimed at redistributing land and improving productivity. Despite some successes, the program in general failed to meet its goals and has undergone continual revision. López Michelsen and Turbay have focused on the Rural Development Program (Desarrollo Rural Integrado), which provides small farmers with the assistance needed to improve their output. This program is still in its initial phase, however, and it is difficult to predict what its results will be. Limited availability of credit, outdated technology, and inefficient land utilization are the major problems to be overcome in the agricultural sector. Colombia has not yet developed a long-term strategy to solve these problems, although numerous govern-

---

[31] "Colombia," *Bank of London and South America Review*, Vol. 15, No. II/81, pp. 92-93.

[32] "Record coffee exports," p. 23.

[33] *Agricultural Situation: Western Hemisphere*, p. 27.

[34] DNP, *Plan de Integración Nacional*, Vol. II, p. 276.

ment agencies exist that focus on parts of the problem.[35] Until a coherent strategy is implemented, the principal export-generating sector of the economy will continue to fluctuate at the mercy of short-term political goals, unavoidable climatic conditions, and international commodity prices.

Manufacturing

The manufacturing sector in Colombia is one of the most dynamic in the economy and is the most attractive to foreign investors. Colombia's manufacturing industries have undergone a radical change in the past three decades. In 1950, four-fifths of Colombian manufacturing was concentrated in consumer goods, while by 1979 intermediate goods accounted for 40 percent of total production and consumer goods had declined to about one-half of total production. The Colombian government followed a policy favoring import substitution in the 1950s and 1960s and shifted to a policy of export promotion in the 1970s when it was realized that few opportunities for import substitution remained and that the domestic market would not grow fast enough to support the desired level of industrial expansion.

The manufacturing sector grew at a faster rate than the overall economy throughout most of the 1970s, and by 1980 manufacturing accounted for about 22 percent of the nation's GDP. Industrial growth and GDP participation figures are presented in Table III-10.

An industrial census carried out in 1976 by the National Statistical Institute revealed that the largest manufacturing industry by value added was the food and beverages industry, which represented 25.2 percent of the total value added in manufacturing. This was followed by the textile industry (14.2 percent), the oil-refining and chemicals industry (11.2 percent), and the pharmaceuticals industry (7.1 percent).[36] The food and beverages industry is also the largest employer among the manufacturing industries, employing about 20 percent of the total manufacturing work force in 1979. Other major employers are the textile industry, the metalworking industry, and the garment industry. The breakdown of the manufacturing work force in 1979 by industry is presented in Table III-11.

---

[35] For a brief description of the different government agencies concerned with agricultural productivity, see *Colombia Today,* Vol. 11, No. 8 (1976).

[36] DNP, *Plan de Integración Nacional,* Vol. II, p. 301.

TABLE III-10
Growth of the Industrial Sector during the 1970s

Year	GDP Growth (%)	Industrial Sector Growth (%)	GDP Participation (%)
1970	6.6	8.5	15.9
1971	5.8	9.3	16.4
1972	9.9	10.1	16.7
1973	7.6	9.6	17.1
1974	6.5	5.8	17.1
1975	4.3	0.2	16.8
1976	4.2	7.7	17.0
1977	4.7	4.2	16.9
1978	8.9	8.5	17.0
1979	5.3	5.3	19.3
1980	4.0	3.7	22.1
1981	2.5	−2.5	n.a.

Sources: Gabriel Poveda Rámos, "Perspectivas del desarrollo industrial en los años ochenta," p. 150, citing Banco de la Republica and Fededesarrollo; *Bank of London and South America Review*, Vol. 15, No. I/81, p. 22; *Colombia Today*, Vol. 16, No. 11 (1981); James W. Wilkie, ed., *Statistical Abstract of Latin America*, Vol. 21 (Los Angeles: UCLA Latin American Center Publications, 1981), p. 279.
n.a. = not available.

TABLE III-11
Employment in Manufacturing by Industry, 1979

Industry	Percent of Total Manufacturing Work Force
Food	14.7
Textiles	14.6
Metalworking and Machinery	13.5
Garments and Footwear	11.1
Chemicals	7.5
Beverages	5.2
Transportation Equipment	4.9
Nonmetallic Minerals	4.0
Printing	3.7
Other	20.8

Source: Departamento Administrativo Nacional de Estadística, cited in *Colombia Today*, Vol. 16, No. 6 (1981).

The productivity of labor in the manufacturing sector increased fairly steadily during the 1970s, as indicated in Figures III-2 and III-3.

FIGURE III-2
Productivity of Labor in Manufacturing
(1974 = 100)

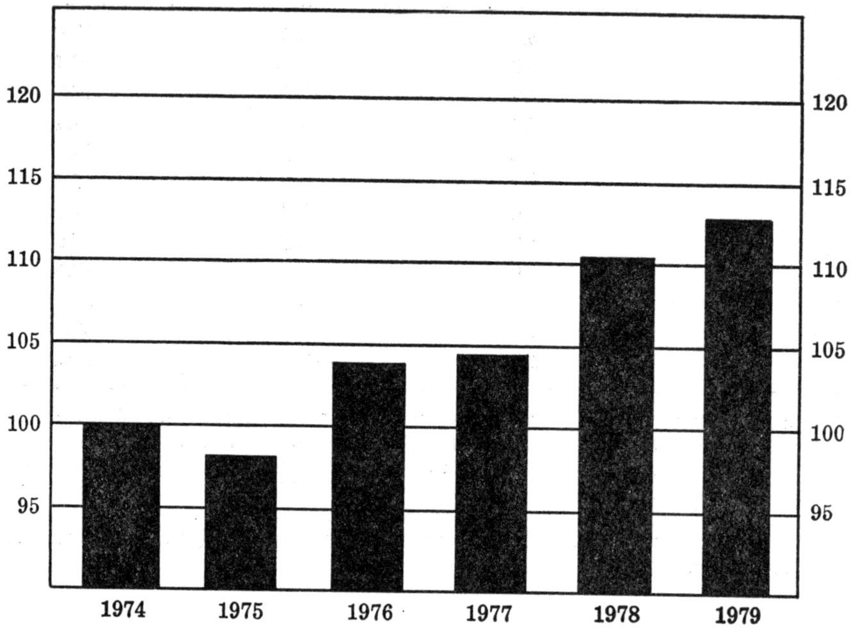

Source: "Colombia—Statistical Survey of the Domestic Economy," *Colombia Today,* Vol. 16, No. 6 (1981).

The vast majority of Colombian manufacturing firms are small. Well over 90 percent of all firms employ fewer than 100 workers, and almost 60 percent of all firms employ fewer than 20 workers. In general, small and medium-sized firms predominate in industries that are labor-intensive. A breakdown of employment distribution in manufacturing by firm size is presented in Table III-12.

The decentralized character of the Colombian economy is reflected in the geographic distribution of manufacturing facilities. Although Bogotá is the largest single industrial area, considerable concentrations of industry also exist in Cali, Medellín, Barranquilla, and Cartagena. Proportionately, Cali is a more heavily industrialized city than Bogotá, with over 30 percent of the work force employed in manufacturing in 1980, compared to 25.2 percent in Bogotá.[37]

FIGURE III-3

Real Manufacturing Output and Employment in Manufacturing

(1974 = 100)

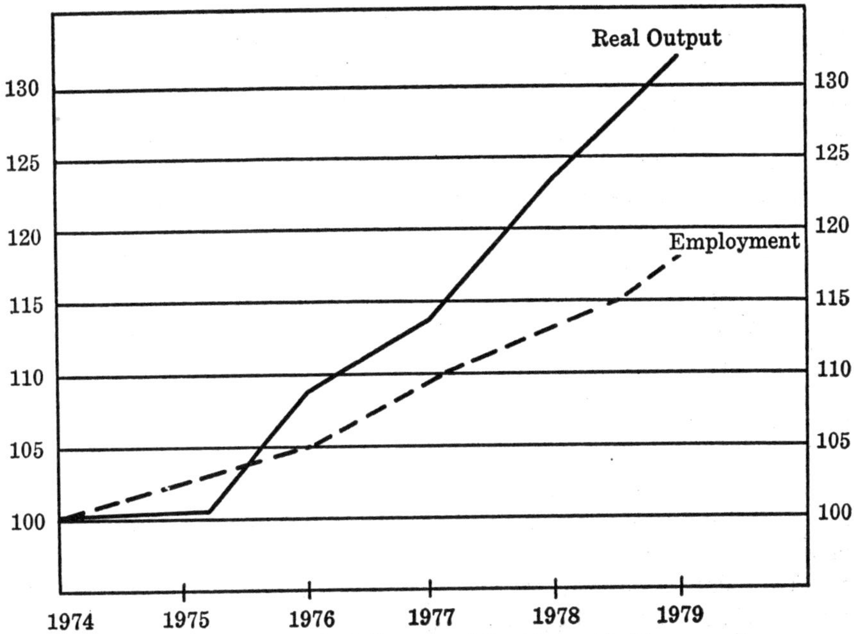

Source: "Colombia—Statistical Survey of the Domestic Economy."

TABLE III-12

Employment Distribution in Manufacturing by Firm Size

Firm Size (number of employees)	Percent of Total Number of Firms	Percent of Total Number of Employees	Average Number of Employees per Firm
Less than 20	57.5	14.3	10
20-49	24.1	18.3	30
50-99	10.1	17.3	65
100-499	7.4	35.7	193
More than 500	0.8	14.5	772

Source: Kyu Sik Lee, "Intra-Urban Location of Manufacturing Employment in Colombia," *World Bank Reprint Series,* No. 195 (Washington, D.C.: World Bank, 1981), p. 224.

[37] Kyu Sik Lee, "Intra-Urban Location of Manufacturing Employment in Colombia," *World Bank Reprint Series,* No. 195 (Washington, D.C.: World Bank, 1981), p. 224.

Colombia produces about 60 percent of the 800,000 metric tons of steel consumed annually.[38] The only fully integrated steel producer is Acerías Paz del Río. Iron ore reserves are 310 million metric tons. The government has a national steel plan (Plan Indicativo Siderúrgico) that aims at supplying 80 percent of domestic demand by 1985. The plan calls for 400,000 metric tons of new capacity to be provided by an expansion of Acerías Paz del Rio, with the remaining increase supplied by semi-integrated plants. This expansion is based on a government estimate that total domestic demand for steel will be 2 million metric tons per year by 1985, which is an optimistic assessment. Expansion of capacity may be hindered by slower than expected growth in demand and by the scarcity of credit.

After considerable expansion in the 1970s, the manufacturing sector faces new and serious challenges in the 1980s. Foreign competition has hurt many industries, and some of the oldest and strongest industries in the manufacturing sector are under severe pressure. Plants are becoming obsolete, and the government's investment plan places little emphasis on public funding of industrial development. In order to sustain growth and avoid supply bottlenecks in the overall development of the economy, the industrial sector will require a considerable yearly investment in the 1980s. With depressed stock prices and high debt-equity ratios—estimated at 60 percent in 1980, up from 37 percent in 1971—internal capital may not suffice to fund the required modernizations and expansions. Colombia's favorable foreign investment climate may partly alleviate the shortage by attracting new foreign capital into manufacturing.

Construction. Construction peaked during the Pastrana administration (1970-1974) because Pastrana's development plan, known as "The Four Strategies," placed heavy emphasis on increasing the activity of the construction sector. The rationale behind Pastrana's program was to expand a sector in which unskilled labor was easily absorbed, thus employing migrant peasants who would normally remain underemployed, at least during their initial months in any urban center to which they migrated. The increased employment was to raise consumption and thus lead to a higher growth rate of the economy. To provide funds for construction work, the government introduced inflation-

[38] "Colombia's Iron and Steel Industry," *Colombia Today,* Vol. 14, No. 1 (1979).

indexed mortgages through the Constant Purchasing Power Unit system.

Construction grew, but the change of administrations in 1974 and the modifications to the system introduced by López Michelsen stalled the growth of the sector after 1974. The sector's performance has been erratic since then. Private-sector construction declined by 8 percent per year between 1978 and 1980, but public-sector construction began to pick up in mid-1979 as work on various Plan de Integración Nacional projects began. The sector recovered as a whole slightly in 1981, buoyed by higher government expenditures on construction and by a slight increase in private activity.[39]

Mining

Under the Colombian Mining Code (Código de Minas), permission to exploit mineral deposits may be granted in three forms: permits issued by the Ministry of Mines and Energy for periods of up to five years, concessions granted for up to thirty years, and association contracts. Certain areas of the country are designated as "national reserves," in which mining can be carried out only by state-owned companies or by joint ventures in which the state holds at least 51 percent of the equity.

In addition to the Cerrejón coal project previously mentioned, a large nickel project is planned for completion in 1985. This project is being carried out by the Cerro Matoso S.A. Corporation, whose principal shareholders are Econiquel (a state-owned enterprise) with 45 percent of the equity, Conicol (representing Chevron and the Hanna Mining Company) with a 20 percent share, and Billiton Overseas Ltd. (a subsidiary of the Royal Dutch Shell Group) with the remaining 35 percent. At projected rates of production, the 19.5 million metric tons of reserves will last twenty-five years. Production is to reach full capacity by 1985; at full capacity, 20,000 tons of ferronickel will be exported yearly to contribute some US$68 million in export earnings. The Hanna Mining Company will manage the project, which will employ 700 men.[40]

---

[39] "Colombia," *Bank of London and South America Review*, Vol. 15, No. IV/81, pp. 211-212.

[40] Carlos Sanclemente, "El Proyecto Minero de Cerro Matoso," *Nueva Frontera*, No. 278 (April 14-20, 1980), pp. 10-11; "Major Nickel and Coal Mining Projects Advanced in Colombia," *Colombia Today*, Vol. 14, No. 2 (1979); "Restructured Project Marks Advance for Colombian Mining Sector," *Business Latin America*, November 28, 1979, pp. 377-78.

Colombia has significant deposits of precious metals, including gold, silver, and platinum. Gold production for the first eleven months of 1981 was 470,875 troy ounces, an increase of 6 percent over 1980; silver production for the same period was 106,576 troy ounces, up 3 percent over 1980; platinum production was 12,260 troy ounces for the same period, up 3 percent over 1980.[41]

Besides the coal and nickel projects, Colombia has deposits of copper, uranium, asbestos, bauxite, and phosphate rock. A feasibility study is under way to determine the profitability of building fertilizer plants to use the 38 million-ton deposits of phosphate rock in northeastern Colombia, and the copper deposits near Mocoa are also being explored to determine their size and their potential for economic exploitation. Similar approaches are being followed with the uranium deposits in the eastern plains and with the bauxite deposits in Cauca.[42] Eternit, the largest Colombian producer of asbestos and cement products, is mining asbestos from the Campamentos reserves in Antioquía.[43]

The main problems facing the mining sector are the difficulties of transportation posed by Colombia's mountainous terrain and by the remoteness of some of the principal deposits from the industrial areas in which the minerals might be profitably processed and used. For this reason, the larger projects (such as the Cerrejón coal project) include considerable investment in infrastructure such as roads, railroads, and ports.

FOREIGN TRADE

The current strength of international reserves can be singled out as one of the most important changes in Colombia's recent economic history. High coffee prices and the inflow of dollars from illegal drug trafficking have pushed the balance on the reserve account above the 5 billion dollar mark, a record never dreamed of twenty years ago.

With the drop of coffee prices in the international market, however, the growth of international reserves is now slowing. On the import side, oil purchases continue to drain the balance of payments. In the years ahead new exports such as coal will

---

41 "Projections for 1982," *Colombia Today,* Vol. 16, No. 11 (1981).

42 DNP, *Plan de Integración Nacional,* Vol. II, pp. 241-47.

43 "Other Mining Projects," *Colombia Today,* Vol. 12, No. 9 (1977).

appear among the major export items, and nontraditional exports are expected to continue their upward trend.

Overview of Recent Policies

Colombian foreign trade policy since World War II can be divided into two clearly identifiable periods. Between 1945 and 1967, exchange and tariff policies were oriented toward substituting imports and developing a solid industrial base. By 1968, Colombian industries supplied 98 percent of the consumer goods demanded by the domestic market; 68 percent of the intermediate goods; 51 percent of the capital goods (including construction materials); and close to 25 percent of machinery and equipment.[44] By the mid-1960s, however, the government was protecting inefficient, capital-intensive industries with very slim chances of competing in the international markets or of effectively substituting for imports.

In 1967, along with making changes in monetary policy, the government of Lleras Restrepo modified the policy governing the external sector. The government began to promote exports by introducing a system of mini-devaluations to reflect the true exchange rate and by providing fiscal incentives such as the Tax Discount Certificates (Certificados de Abono Tributario—CAT) and the Plan Vallejo.[45]

Since 1967, the system has been gradually liberalized. Recently steps have been taken to simplify customs procedures.[46] In 1979, to some extent pressed by bountiful exchange earnings, the government reduced tariffs on automobiles, motorcycles, and certain electronic goods.[47] Finally, the exchange-control system was relaxed so that companies could open foreign currency accounts to finance business trips abroad and to pay stipends and fees. Restrictions were also lifted on "medical, food and communication expenses, payments to students abroad, the $6000 limit for

---

[44] Guillermo E. Perry, "Politica Cambiaria y de Comercio Exterior: Revisión de la Experiencia Histórica y Propuesta para la Próxima Década. Bogotá Julio, de 1978," in *La Economía Colombiana en la Década de los Ochenta,* p. 281.

[45] The Plan Vallejo eliminated tariffs on raw materials that had to be imported to manufacture exportable goods.

[46] "Colombia's New Rules for Customs Procedures Will Facilitate Imports," *Business Latin America,* June 27, 1979, p. 202.

[47] "Colombia Reduces Tariffs," *Business Latin America,* July 11, 1979, p. 221.

travelers, subscriptions to publications and expenses for books."[48] The 20 percent reserve requirement on banks' foreign exchange accounts was also abolished.

The exchange rate has also been used to promote exports. After the temporary stagnation of exports between 1975 and 1976, the government accelerated the devaluation rate to 5 percent in 1977, 6.3 in 1978, 10.7 in 1979, and 16 percent in 1980 to sustain Colombian competitiveness in world markets. The peso still remains overvalued, however, and important sectors such as the textile industry are taking severe losses.

Exports

Coffee still generates about one-half of the total export income (see Table III-13). If illegal exports were factored into official exports, they would trail coffee as the second or third generator of foreign exchange.

Over 65 percent of Colombian exports are agricultural goods. Nontraditional exports are mostly manufactured products. The

TABLE III-13
Colombian Foreign Trade
(US$ millions)

Type	1978	1979	1980	1981
Exports	3,088	3,672	4,226	3,270
Coffee	2,011	2,005	2,360	1,374
Textiles/Garments	167	136	258	236
Fuel Oil (and other refined products)	126	140	239	266
Bananas	75	85	108	136
Cut Flowers	53	79	102	110
Cotton Fiber	73	52	102	96
Imports	3,412	4,629	5,412	6,094
Durable Consumer	99	251	400	445
Nondurable Consumer	198	284	292	325
Raw Materials/ Intermediate Goods	1,639	2,383	2,695	3,111
Capital Goods	1,456	1,669	1,991	2,173

Sources: "Colombia—Basic Data & Economic Indicators," *Colombia Today,* Vol. 14, No. 5 (1981); *ibid.,* Vol. 17, No. 1 (1982); *Bank of London and South America Review,* Vol. 16, No. I/82, p. 33.

[48] "Bogotá Eases Exchange Controls," *Business Latin America,* June 11, 1980, p. 187.

textile industry's contribution to exports, after peaking in 1974, is going downhill due to high costs and plant obsolescence. During 1980 exports reached $3.4 billion, bringing the balance of trade to a deficit of US$200 million. For 1981, coffee revenues declined to $1.6 billion as prices dipped; nontraditional exports increased by 2 percent to $681 million. The higher oil bill and the drop in coffee income produced a trade deficit of US$937 million for 1981. The deficit on the current account for all of 1981 was estimated at $646 million; the estimated capital account surplus of US$861 million produced an estimated overall balance of payments surplus of $215 million.[49]

The United States has seen its share of Colombian exports drop from 37.9 percent in 1973 to 24.5 percent in 1979; however, the United States remains the major destination of Colombian exports. Other major buyers of Colombian exports are West Germany and Venezuela. The latter has become the chief purchaser of Colombian durable consumer goods, construction materials, machinery, equipment, and other capital goods. Exports to developed economies are mostly agricultural goods (coffee, bananas, cut flowers), together with some final consumer goods such as garments and frozen shrimp.[50]

Imports

Imports grew at an annual rate of 6 percent between 1970 and 1978. Refined and crude oil imports have increased as a percentage of imports from 0.3 percent in 1973 (when Colombia was still a net oil exporter) to 14.5 percent in 1979. Major import suppliers are the United States, Japan, Germany, and France. Among the Andean Pact members, Venezuela and Ecuador are selling more goods now in Colombia than ever before. Overall imports from Latin America increased from 13.9 percent in 1974 to 17.0 percent of the total in 1979. During that same period, imports from Europe dropped from 30.7 to 24.6 percent. Imports consist mostly of raw materials and intermediate goods, including oil products. Capital goods, primarily for use in industry and transportation, accounted for one-third of the imports during the period. Consumer goods remained stable, in-

---

[49] *Colombia Today,* Vol. 16, No. 11 (1981).

[50] "Colombia—Basic Data and Economic Indicators," *ibid.,* Vol. 16, No. 7 (1981).

creasing their participation in 1978 when domestic crops were poor.

Balance of Payments

Table III-14 shows the Colombian balance of payments and the balance of international reserves for the years between 1965 and 1980. This table illustrates the drastic change that occurred during the 1970s when the balance on the international reserve account soared. Total foreign debt at the end of 1980 was US$4,025 million.[51] The reserves available then would have been enough to liquidate the entire foreign debt.

TABLE III-14

Balance of Payments by Item, 1965-1981

(US$ millions)

Item	1965	1970	1975	1979	1980	1981
Current Inflows	496	800	1,789	4,623	5,654	4,986
Coffee	347	406	635	1,769	1,981	1,561
Other Exports	n.a.	n.a.	n.a.	1,275	1,413	1,364
Petroleum Investments	n.a.	n.a.	n.a.	52	85	87
Services/ Transfers	n.a.	n.a.	n.a.	1,453	1,864	1,734
Current Outflows	387	859	1,759	3,488	4,919	5,633
Petroleum Imports	n.a.	n.a.	26	571	622	n.a.
Other Imports	n.a.	n.a.	1,733	2,917	4,297	n.a.
Services/ Transfers	n.a.	n.a.	n.a.	852	1,307	1,674
Current Account Balance	109	−59	30	1,135	735	−647
Capital Account Balance	−47	114	88	486	572	861
Variation in Gross Reserves	n.a.	n.a.	n.a.	1,620	1,307	213
Balance of International Reserves	n.a.	152	547	4,113	5,420	5,633

Sources: "Perspectivas Económicas 1981," *Documentos Nueva Frontera*, No. 53 (February 1981), p. 18; *Financial Times*, February 19, 1982, p. 28.

n.a. = not available.

[51] *Bank of London and South America Review*, Vol. 15, No. IV/81, p. 214.

FOREIGN INVESTMENT

Colombia welcomes foreign investment but also carefully scrutinizes proposals to make sure that they agree with development plans and meet legal requirements. The areas in which foreign investment is encouraged and those in which it is prohibited are well specified. Manufacturing activities and mining, including oil and gas, are favored sectors for investment. Foreign investment is prohibited in public utilities, insurance, domestic transport, advertising, broadcasting, television, and newspapers and magazines, and it is limited in finance and banking.[52]

Investment proposals for the oil and gas sector enjoy preferential treatment and are handled by the Ministry of Mines and Energy. All other proposals must be approved by the National Planning Department. Colombia adheres to the Andean Group Statute on Foreign Investment and has gradually liberalized many of the restrictive policies originally embraced by the Cartagena Agreement to make investment in Colombia more attractive.

Regulation of Foreign Investment

Decision 24, which was promulgated by the Andean Pact, was formally implemented in Colombia by Decrees 1900 and 2719 of 1973.[53] Its provisions have since been modified. (See Table III-15 for highlights of and amendments to Decision 24.) In 1977, Colombia adopted the Andean Pact's Decision 103, which increased the ceilings on remittance of profits and reinvestment of undistributed profits. Decree 1161 of 1979 established a "fade-out" schedule for the reduction of foreign equity to minority status, and stated the conditions under which foreign investors could be classified as Colombians.[54]

For investment purposes, Colombia acknowledges three types of enterprises, distinguished by the participation rate of domestic capital (see Table III-15). Colombia encourages the formation of joint ventures by offering special benefits to mixed enterprises, such as the possibility of using development funds ("fondos de fomento") and the opportunity of benefiting from the expanded market of the Andean Group nations.

---

[52] "Foreign Investment Guidelines," *Colombia Today*, Vol. 14, No. 11 (1979).

[53] "Uniform Treatment of Foreign Capital," *Colombia Today*, Vol. 10, No. 11 (1975).

[54] "Colombia Issues Clarifying Regulations on Ancom Rules," *Business Latin America*, June 20, 1979, p. 194.

Investment in Colombia

Among those sectors screened by the National Planning Department, the manufacturing sector holds the largest share of foreign investment, with over 70 percent of the total invested through 1980. The other sector that has traditionally attracted foreign investment is the oil industry. In the 1980s, mining should attract an increasing proportion of foreign investment as

TABLE III-15

Summary of Foreign Investment Regulations

Enterprise Classification:	National: less than 20 percent foreign equity. Mixed: between 20 and 50 percent foreign equity. Foreign: more than 50 percent foreign equity.
Divestment:	Enterprises formed after January 1, 1974, must reduce foreign equity to below 50 percent according to the following schedule: —85 percent maximum initial foreign equity —70 percent maximum foreign equity after 5 years —55 percent maximum foreign equity after 10 years —49 percent maximum foreign equity after 15 years The following activities are exempt from the fade-out requirement: —hydrocarbons, mining, and forestry —tourist enterprises in which Colombian capital is less than 15 percent —industries exporting over 80 percent of their output to Andean Pact countries Enterprises in existence before January 1, 1974, are not required to divest; however, unless they divest they are not eligible for tariff reductions between Andean Pact countries.
Investors' Rights:	—Profits may be remitted up to 20 percent of investment per year. —Capital and capital gains may be remitted after liquidation or selling out. —Profits exceeding 20 percent may be capitalized at a rate of 7 percent. —Profits above 20 percent may be reinvested as new investment if 50 percent of the reinvested profits are used to purchase Institute of Industrial Development certificates. —No profit remittance ceiling on hydrocarbon enterprises.

Source: Business International Corporation, "Colombia," *Investing, Licensing and Trading Conditions Abroad,* October 1979, pp. 2-16.

the Cerrejón and Cerro Matoso projects begin operation. Table III-16 summarizes foreign investment by sector.

The United States continues to be the largest single source of foreign investment in Colombia, with about 53 percent of the total direct foreign investment as of 1980. Table III-17 presents the sources and amounts of direct foreign investment in the Colombian economy.

TABLE III-16

Direct Foreign Investment by Economic Activity

(millions of US$)

Activity	Accumulated Investment (1980)	Percent	New Investment (1981)
Manufacturing	749.8	70.6	104
Financial Sector	110.2	10.3	10
Retail and Wholesale Trade, Hotels, and Restaurants	96.3	9.0	9
Mining (except oil and gas)	53.6	5.0	16
Transportation, Communications	32.1	3.0	n.a.
Agriculture, Fishing, Forestry	11.1	1.0	n.a.
Other	7.7	1.0	n.a.
Total	1,060.8	100.0	166

Source: "Colombia: A Statistical Survey of the International Economy," *Colombia Today*, Vol. 16, No. 7 (1981); *Bank of London and South America Review*, Vol. 16, No. I/82, p. 32.

n.a. = not available.

THE "OTHER" ECONOMY

It has long been recognized that illegal activities, such as smuggling and drug trafficking, are major unmeasured factors in the Colombian economy. For obvious reasons, official statistical data on this subject are scarce. The extent of illegal activities and their effect both on employment and on the internal capital market is therefore very difficult to assess; however, a recent study by two Colombian researchers, Caballero and Junguito, attempts a fairly scientific evaluation of the effect of the underground economy on the availability of capital for legitimate investment.[55] More recently, the National Association of Financial Institutions (Asociación Nacional de Instituciones Financieras—ANIF) has undertaken several studies to evaluate the economic

[55] Roberto Junguito Bonnet and Carlos Caballero Argáez, "La Otra Economía," *Coyuntura Económica*, Vol. VIII, No. 4 (December 1978), pp. 103-39.

TABLE III-17
Foreign Investment by Country of Origin, 1979 [a]
(millions of US$)

Country	Investment
United States	459.4
Switzerland	61.2
Panama	59.5
France	33.4
Canada	30.0
Venezuela	26.2
Great Britain	25.8
Netherlands	23.0
Dutch Antilles	20.7
Ecuador	17.6
Sweden	14.3
Japan	10.6
Bahamas	10.4
Total Investment	864.9

Source: Mimeograph released by the Banco de la República, August 1979.
[a] Does not include investments in the petroleum industry.

impact of the drug trade. The following description draws heavily on the initial work by Caballero and Junguito.

The "other" economy can be subdivided into what Caballero and Junguito labeled the informal economy and the illegal economy. The informal economy takes in mostly artisans, small farmers, unregistered construction workers, and participants in other nonregistered activities that are not included on the national accounts. The most significant impact, however, comes from the illegal economy, which includes activities such as illegal export of traditional products like coffee and cattle; exports of marijuana and cocaine; overbilling or underbilling of exports and imports; illegal import, primarily of cigarettes, liquor, appliances, cosmetics, toys, crystal, canned foods, watches, fabrics, and clothing;[56] and the black market in dollars.

Using publicly available information and assuming an annual marijuana production of 40,000 or 70,000 pounds, Caballero and Junguito have drawn conclusions about the distribution of total income among the various participants in marijuana trafficking. Under both alternatives (40,000 or 70,000 pounds), Colombians end up with 2.7 percent of the total income. This percentage

[56] Junguito Bonnet and Caballero Argáez, "La Otra Economía," p. 127.

would represent a potential inflow of $432 or $756 million, depending on which alternative is selected. Assuming revenues of US$500 million, net income would be US$130 million once production costs are subtracted. At 1976 prices, this sum would be equivalent to 2.7 percent of the nation's GDP.

Colombia is not a producer of cocaine, but it processes most of the cocaine coming from Peru and Bolivia. According to the U.S. Embassy in Bogotá, 70 to 90 percent of the 15-20 tons of cocaine consumed annually in the United States is processed in Colombia. Based on this estimate, Caballero and Junguito estimated revenues to Colombians (excluding profits taken by distributors in the United States) at US$154 million. When production costs are discounted, net income from cocaine processing would represent 0.9 percent of GDP.[57]

Drug exports and the smuggling of goods to other countries are the principal sources of illegal funds in the "other" economy. A significant proportion of illegal funds from these activities probably remains abroad; for the funds that are absorbed into the legal economy, the principal ways of "officializing" illegal cash are overbilling tourist services and exports and underbilling imports. Caballero and Junguito estimate that illegal exports increased threefold between 1974 and 1977, and that the value of illegal exports is increasing faster than the value of legal exports.

Caballero and Junguito hypothesize that the low savings and tax rates in Colombia can be explained by the existence of a parallel capital market. Part of this market is under government control (the "informal" sector) and is known as the "nonbanking" market; the other part corresponds to funds generated by illegal activities and "laundered" in the ways mentioned above. The existence of large sums of unrecorded illegal funds in the economy necessarily alters interest rates and the availability of funds in the legal capital market.

EMPLOYMENT AND WAGES

Employment

Figures on the composition of the economically active population are presented in Table III-18. Information on current employment levels and conditions is available from the periodic surveys taken by the National Bureau of Statistics (Departamento Administrativo Nacional de Estadística). Information on rural

[57] *Ibid.*, p. 122.

TABLE III-18

Economically Active Population by Economic Sector

(thousands)

Sector	1970 Population	1970 Percent	1980 Population	1980 Percent
Agriculture	2,427.0	47.2	2,095.5	33.0
Services	925.9	18.0	1,086.4	17.2
Trade and Finance	440.5	8.6	766.9	12.1
Manufacturing	655.9	12.8	749.5	11.9
Construction	220.7	4.3	248.4	3.9
Transportation, Communications	191.8	3.7	217.1	3.4
Mining	81.2	1.6	44.8	0.7
Utilities	13.2	0.3	25.4	0.3
Other and Unemployed	177.9	3.5	1,084.1	29.6
Total	5,134.1	100.0	6,318.6	100.0

Sources: International Labour Organisation, *Yearbook of Labour Statistics, 1971* (Geneva: International Labour Office, 1971), p. 67; *ibid., 1981*, p. 138.

workers is scarce and mostly outdated. A figure illustrating the changes in Colombia's population structure that are projected to take place by the year 2000 is presented in Appendix A.

The composition of the Colombian work force is being changed not only by demographic factors such as the declining birth rate, but also by social factors similar to those existing in other countries, such as the increasing participation of women in the labor market. Between 1970 and 1978, the participation rate of women in the labor market increased from 29.8 percent to 31.6 percent.[58]

Government statistics on employment generation in urban areas are presented in Table III-19. The number of jobs generated by

TABLE III-19

Urban Employment Generation by Sector

(percent)

Sector	1971-1974	1974-1978
Manufacturing	25.4	36.3
Trade	30.8	24.6
Services	31.0	23.2
Other	12.8	15.9

Source: DNP, *Plan de Integración Nacional,* Vol. II, p. 335.

[58] DNP, *Plan de Integración Nacional,* Vol. II, p. 331.

the mining sector will probably increase in the 1980s as the two large mining projects are brought on stream. Manufacturing, however, is facing difficulties, which will probably prevent a recurrence of the significant expansion in employment that occurred between 1974 and 1978.

As part of a study of the future of the Colombian economy, the Colombian government made forecasts of the future labor supply taking into consideration the demographic changes mentioned above. Two sets of assumptions were used to evaluate two possible alternatives: a "high" alternative based on a declining fertility rate and an increasing life expectancy, and a "low" alternative based on the same increased life expectancy but a sharper decline in fertility. The statistical projections of this study are presented in Appendix B, Tables B-1 and B-2, respectively. Under either alternative, the yearly increase in the size of the labor market will reach a peak in the period 1980-1985, when children born before the birth rate started to decline in 1964 enter the work force. After 1985, the increase in the size of the work force should moderate, although it should still be higher than the increases experienced between 1964 and 1973.[59] The implications of these projections for economic policy are obvious: activities that generate jobs will require increasing attention and promotion from the government.

According to government statistics, unemployment averaged between 7 and 10 percent of the work force between 1970 and 1978. The reliability of official unemployment statistics is open to question, however, because of the large number of workers employed in the "informal sector" of the economy. The "informal sector" is defined by the government to include the self-employed, domestic servants, and those workers employed by industrial establishments with fewer than ten workers. The "informal" labor force in urban areas represents approximately 45 percent of the total employed population.[60] A statistical breakdown of the Colombian work force by "modern" and "informal" sectors, together

---

59 Hernando Gomez Buendia, "Perspectivas Ocupacionales," *La Economía Colombiana en la Decada de los Ochenta*, p. 69.

60 DNP, *Plan de Integración Nacional*, Vol. II, p. 342.

with wage differentials between the two sectors, is presented in Table III-20.

TABLE III-20

Wage Differentials between "Modern" and "Informal" Sectors, 1979 [a]

Category of Worker	Monthly Income Informal Sector (current pesos)	Monthly Income Modern Sector (current pesos)	Informal Sector as Percent of Modern Sector
Sex			
Men	3,024	5,073	60
Women	1,663	3,080	53
Total	2,375	4,476	53
Age			
20 to 30 years	1,805	2,993	60
30 to 40 years	2,452	4,950	49
40 to 65 years	2,277	9,280	24
Education			
None	1,281	1,674	77
Grade School	1,819	2,060	88
High School	3,776	3,673	103
University	3,656	9,328	39

Source: DNP, *Plan de Integración*, p. 344, citing F. Bourgignon, "Pobreza y dualismo en el sector urbano en las economías en desarrollo: el caso de Colombia," *Desarrollo y Sociedad*, January 1979.

[a] Informal Sector refers to enterprises employing fewer than ten workers.

Wages

Table III-21 presents changes in real wages for workers in manufacturing industries. In general, wages in manufacturing increased in real terms in the 1960s and declined in real terms in the 1970s. The evolution of the minimum wage also reflects this downward trend in real wages, as indicated in Table III-22 and in Figure III-4. The purchasing power of the minimum wage declined by 8 percent between 1970 and 1980.

The declines in real wages in the course of the past decade may bring increased labor unrest as workers struggle to recuperate their salaries' lost purchasing power. For example, the government-decreed increase of 26.5 percent in the minimum wage that went into effect on January 1, 1981, was widely criticized by trade union leaders as insufficient; several union leaders demanded an increase of up to 50 percent.[61] Dissatisfaction over

[61] "Colombia," *Bank of London and South America Review*, Vol. 15, No. I/81 (February 1981), p. 22.

TABLE III-21
Changes in Real Remuneration by Economic Activity
(percent)

Activity	Change 1962-1969	Change 1970-1979
Manufacturing—Blue-Collar		
Unskilled		
Food	+22.2%	−0.4%
Tobacco	−13.0%	−23.8%
Clothing and Shoes	+1.1%	+9.9%
Lumber	+0.5%	−6.0%
Furniture	+0.4%	−11.0%
Leather	+20.5%	−8.1%
Metalworking	+5.5%	−1.2%
Skilled		
Petroleum	−0.8%	−26.2%
Beverages	+0.6%	−8.0%
Textiles	+23.1%	−12.9%
Paper	+33.2%	+6.2%
Rubber	+27.1%	−0.6%
Metalworking	+37.8%	−25.8%
Manufacturing—White-Collar		
Construction Manager	+7.1%	+17.6%
Nonprofessional (with 15 yrs. experience) (financial sector)	+43.9%	−7.0%
Professional (financial sector)	+18.1%	−20.6%
Government Workers		
Professional	−21.6%	−32.9%
Primary School Teacher	n.a.	+2.7%
High School Teacher	n.a.	−5.4%

Source: "El impacto de los salarios," *El Espectador,* March 23, 1981, p. 7A, citing Fedesarrollo calculations.
n.a. = not available.

wage scales led to a wave of strikes in mid-1981,[62] and the government seems to be responding by including unions and businessmen in the decision-making process on minimum wage increases. The increases that went into effect in January of 1982 (30 percent for urban workers, 32 percent for rural workers) were arrived at through tripartite negotiations among labor, business,

[62] "Colombia: Summary of the Current Situation," p. 210.

TABLE III-22
Real Minimum Wages, 1970-1980

Year	Minimum Wage (current pesos)	Minimum Wage (constant 1970 pesos)
1970	619	619
1972	660	530
1974	1,200	630
1976	1,560	555
1977	2,340	640
1978	2,580	534
1979	3,450	550
1980	4,500	569

Source: "El impacto de los salarios," p. 7A.

and government. Union leaders had demanded a 40 percent increase to recover purchasing power lost in previous years, although the increase in the 1981 CPI was 26.4 percent.[63]

THE NATIONAL INTEGRATION PLAN

In the preceding description of the Colombian economy, frequent reference has been made to the Plan de Integración Nacional (PIN), a comprehensive plan for economic development. In this section, the development goals and investment objectives of the plan will be described, together with an evaluation of the degree to which the plan's objectives have been reached.

In an analysis of the economy, the National Planning Department pointed out the following critical problems.[64]

—Colombia's emergence since 1975 as an oil importer, compounded by a significant reduction in proven reserves.

—Stagnation and negative growth rates of the mining sector since the early 1970s.

—The reduction since 1975 of public investment in real terms.

—The disrepair of the railroad system.

—The deficit in the generation of electrical energy despite the efforts made in recent years.

[63] "Colombia Unveils New Minimums," *Business Latin America*, January 20, 1982, p. 19.

[64] "El Plan de Integración Nacional," *Nueva Frontera*, No. 286 (June 9-15, 1980), p. 7.

FIGURE III-4

Changes in Real Legal Minimum Wage, 1970-1979

(constant 1977 pesos)

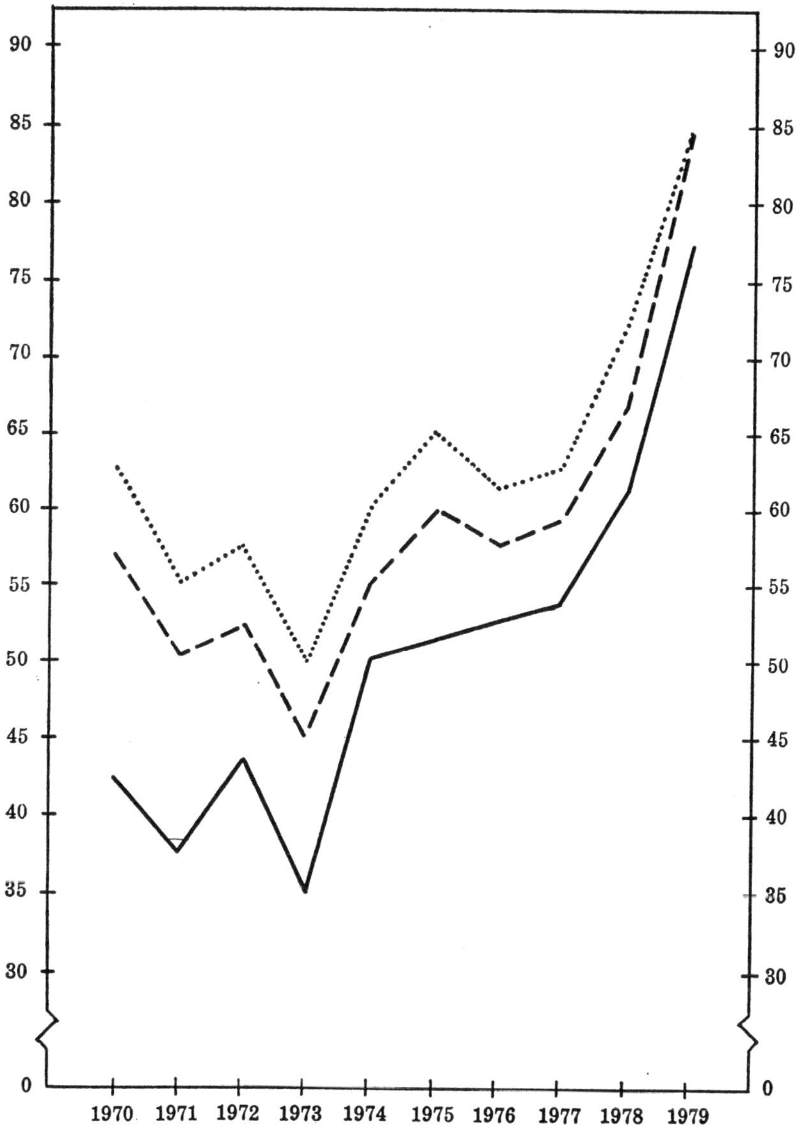

Key: ———————Minimum wage of rural workers

– – – – – – Minimum wage of workers in medium-sized cities

........................Minimum wage of workers in large cities

Source: DNP, *Plan de Integración Nacional,* Vol. II, p. 346.

According to this analysis, the PIN was drawn up to meet the following objectives:

—economic decentralization of regional autonomy,

—development of the energy and mining sectors,

—improvement of the transportation and communication systems, and

—development of a new social policy.

The rationale behind this set of objectives is to facilitate the government's handling of the economy by placing more responsibility at the regional and municipal levels. At the same time, the improvement of the transportation and communication systems will facilitate the exchange of goods and services among the different regions of the country, thus expanding each individual market and the overall market potential of the nation. To finance the investments required to expand the market, the government needs funds that to some extent must come from abroad by means of export payments or borrowings.

On the social front, the PIN aims at solving the ever-present problems of high infant mortality rates, school attrition rates and low educational quality, and widespread underemployment. It also is geared to improving other, more contemporary problems, such as infant neglect due to women's increased involvement in the work force, and the serious problems arising in overcrowded cities such as Bogotá.

The social sector was given the highest priority among PIN investments, with 37 percent of the total outlays. Electricity projects, the delay of which could thwart the overall development effort, will receive 19 percent. The transportation and communication systems will get close to 17 percent for the improvement of roads, railways, and ports. Development of hydrocarbons and mining is targeted to receive about 15 percent of the budgeted investment. A slim 4 percent is scheduled for agricultural projects. The total bill adds up to US$22 billion, of which US$6.8 billion (30.1 percent) is scheduled to be financed from international sources.[65]

In mid-1981 the government released a report detailing the achievements under the plan. This report showed high rates of

---

[65] *Quarterly Economic Review of Colombia and Ecuador* (London: The Economist Intelligence Unit), Third Quarter 1980, p. 10.

completion in the coal sector (actual spending was 201 percent of planned spending), child care (152 percent), health programs (122 percent), and rural development (103 percent). In the critical sectors that the PIN was designed to improve (infrastructure, energy, and mining), however, the completion rate was much lower. The overall completion rate for the energy and mining sector was 76 percent, while communications spending was only 58 percent of target. Other particularly weak areas were the National Food and Nutrition Plan (48 percent) and the Industrial Parks Plan (66 percent). The overall completion rate for all spending areas was 83 percent. Financing seems to be the primary bottleneck: US$5 billion has already been invested in projects under the plan, but a further US$16 billion will be required between 1982 and 1984 if the plan's goals are to be fully met.[66]

Despite the relatively high level of overall completion, the PIN does not appear to be stimulating the economy to the extent that its formulators had hoped. The contraction in industrial activity in 1981 is an indication that many problems remain to be addressed.

CONCLUSION

The Colombian economy is fairly diversified and has good prospects for steady growth in the 1980s. The economy's major problems are an excessive reliance on coffee for export income, the obsolescence of many industrial facilities, and the relative stagnation of the agricultural sector. On the positive side, political stability and the pro-investment policies of President Betancur could attract the foreign investment needed to revitalize industry and promote overall growth.

---

[66] "Colombia Claims High Completion Rate," pp. 258-59.

CHAPTER IV

Labor Law and Labor Relations in Colombia

The general principles of Colombian labor law are based upon provisions of the National Constitution of 1886. Article 17 states:

> Labor is a social obligation and shall enjoy the special protection of the state.[1]

The constitution goes further to provide that the common good supersedes the rights of individuals and that property is a social relationship that implies obligations.[2] With respect to the right to work, the constitution states that individuals are free to choose their profession or occupation. The state, however, retains the right to set standards of efficiency and qualifications and may regulate the practice of a profession.[3]

The state also plays a major role in directing the productive capabilities of the country and in providing employment in conjunction with a policy designed to ensure economic development and social justice.

> Freedom of enterprise and private initiative are guaranteed within the limits of the common welfare, but the general direction of the economy shall be the responsibility of the state. The state shall intervene, by mandate of the law, in the production, distribution, utilization, and consumption of public and private goods and services, so as to rationalize and plan the economy and to achieve overall development.
>
> The state shall also intervene, by mandate of the law, to give full employment to human and natural resources, following an income and wage policy according to which the principal objective

---

[1] Organization of American States, *Constitution of the Republic of Colombia 1886*, Legislative Act of 1936, Article 17 (Washington, D.C.: OAS General Secretariat, 1971), p. 7.

[2] *Ibid.*, Article 30, p. 9.

[3] *Ibid.*, Article 39, p. 10.

of economic development is social justice and the harmonious betterment of the community as a whole, and particularly the working classes.[4]

THE LABOR CODE

The Labor Code (Código Sustantivo de Trabajo) was enacted in 1950. It represents a collection of previous social and labor legislation which until the enactment of the Labor Code was contained in a wide variety of laws and executive decrees. The scope of the Labor Code is very broad, although it also includes provisions that apply only to particular occupations or that concern specialized fringe benefits not applicable to all workers. The general provisions of the Labor Code apply to all workers regardless of nationality. All workers are considered equal before the law, and there is no jurisdictional distinction between white-collar and blue-collar workers.

The Labor Code states that its provisions are to be interpreted liberally in favor of the worker. When civil law is found to be in conflict with the Labor Code, the Labor Code prevails, and when disputes arise over the application of two different provisions of the Labor Code, the provision most favorable to the worker is to be applied.

The Labor Code is divided into two major sections: Book I and Book II. Book I describes the minimum standards that must be observed by employers with respect to hours of work, wages, vacations, and fringe benefits. The code explicitly states that its standards are the minimum, and that individual labor contracts may differ from the standards only if they provide improved benefits or working conditions.

Book II of the Labor Code contains regulations concerning labor unions and collective bargaining. In general, its provisions are favorable to existing unions and to the organization of new unions. The important provisions of both books of the Labor Code are described in detail in succeeding sections of this chapter.

Major modifications to the original Labor Code have been made by a series of laws and executive decrees. The most important single modification was a general reform of the code, which was enacted in 1968 (Law 48). Table IV-1 presents the major modifications of the original code that have been enacted since 1950, as well as other important laws and decrees related to labor matters.

---

[4] *Ibid.*, Article 32 (Article 6, Legislative Act of 1968), p. 9.

TABLE IV-1
Major Labor Code Amendments and Supplementary Labor Statutes

Statute	Number	Date	Subject
Decree	2553	1951	Education of workers' children
Resolution	206	1951	Severance pay and workers' life insurance
Decree	53	1952	Nonprofit undertakings
Decree	1489	1952	Trade union supervision
Resolution	4	1952	Trade union constitution
Decree-law	2318	1953	Employment agencies
Decree	8	1954	Agricultural workers
Decree	2240	1954	Employment of foreigners
Decree	85	1956	Trade unions
Decree-law	1393	1956	Workers' national service obligation
Decree	118	1957	National Apprenticeship Service
Decree	1521	1957	Family allowances regulation
Law	15	1958	Employment of the middle-aged
Law	15	1959	Workers' daily transportation subsidy
Law	187	1959	National Wage Council
Law	188	1959	Apprenticeship
Decree	1593	1959	Bank strikes
Resolution	242	1959	Periodic reports
Decree	1256	1960	Employment of the middle-aged, regulation
Decree	2838	1960	Apprenticeship contracts
Decree	2968	1960	Workers' mutual funds
Law	171	1961	Pensions
Decree	958	1961	Workers' mutual fund regulation
Decree	1952	1961	Collective bargaining
Decree	3151	1962	Family allowances
Decree	3378	1962	Right of association
Decree	2497	1963	Mass dismissal
Law	58	1963	Family allowances
Decree	1598	1963	Withholding and deductions
Decree	2937	1964	Family allowance funds
Decree	13	1965	Hours of work
Decree	2351	1965	Labor Code reform
Decree	2352	1965	Night work
Decree	99	1965	Public services
Law	4	1966	Pensions
Law	73	1966	Maternity and child protection
Decree-law	1666	1966	National Employment Service
Decree	939	1966	Strikes
Decree	1373	1966	Labor Code reform
Decree	2258	1966	Labor disputes
Decree	2922	1966	Bonus
Law	63	1967	Supplementary benefits
Decree	13	1967	Days of rest
Decree	245	1967	Family allowances
Decree	423	1967	Severance pay

TABLE IV-1 (continued)

Statute	Number	Date	Subject
Law	48	1968	Labor Code reform
Decree	995	1968	Holidays with pay
Decree	3135	1968	Public employees' benefits
Decree	3136	1968	Ministry of Labor
Decree	1233	1969	Minimum wage
Law	3	1969	Supplementary benefits
Decree	443	1969	Labor law enforcement
Decree	1848	1969	Public-sector workers
Decree	825	1970	Supplementary benefits
Resolution	1590	1970	Family allowances
Decree	276	1971	Strikes under state of siege
Decree	884	1971	Pensions
Decree	433	1971	Social security
Decree	434	1971	Public-employee benefits
Decree	435	1971	Public-employee benefits
Decree	577	1972	Minimum wage
Law	10	1972	Private-sector pensions
Decree	671	1972	Collective agreements
Decree	2486	1973	Sanctions for illegal work delay
Decree	2373	1974	Family subsidy for peasants
Law	27	1974	Day-care centers
Law	52	1975	Interest accrued on severance pay
Decree	2004	1977	Strikes under state of siege
Decree	1469	1978	Union organization and strikes

Sources: U.S. Department of Labor, *Labor Law and Practice in Colombia,* BLS Report No. 408 (Washington, D.C.: U.S. Government Printing Office, 1972), pp. 79-80; Jorge Ortega Torres, ed., *Código Sustantivo del Trabajo y Código Procesal del Trabajo, 1972-1979* (Bogotá: Editorial Temis, 1979), pp. 570-1,008.

As a member of the International Labor Organization (ILO), Colombia has ratified many of its conventions. Such provisions have been incorporated into current labor legislation. Table IV-2 presents a detailed listing of those ILO conventions that have been ratified by Colombia.

Efforts made by both the López Michelsen and Turbay governments to introduce labor reforms faced stiff opposition from labor leaders and congress and therefore had to be shelved.

THE MINISTRY OF LABOR

The Ministry of Labor and Social Security (Ministerio de Trabajo y Seguridad Social) is divided into departments dealing with industrial medicine, occupational health and safety, individual labor matters, collective labor matters (i.e., supervision of unions), female and child labor, and rural affairs. The minister of labor appoints regional labor inspectors who are authorized

TABLE IV-2

ILO Conventions Ratified by Colombia as of 1981

Convention Number	Title	Date
1	Hours of Work (Industry)	1919
2	Unemployment	1919
3	Maternity Protection	1919
4	Night Work (Women)	1919
5	Minimum Age (Industry)	1919
7	Minimum Age (Sea)	1920
8	Unemployment Indemnity (Shipwreck)	1920
9	Placing of Seamen	1920
11	Right of Association (Agriculture)	1921
12	Workmen's Compensation (Agriculture)	1921
13	White Lead (Painting)	1921
14	Weekly Rest (Industry)	1921
15	Minimum Age (Trimmers and Stokers)	1921
16	Medical Examination of Young Persons (Sea)	1921
17	Workmen's Compensation (Accidents)	1925
18	Workmen's Compensation (Occupational Diseases)	1925
19	Equality of Treatment (Accident Compensation)	1925
20	Night Work (Bakeries)	1925
21	Inspection of Emigrants	1926
22	Seamen's Articles of Agreement	1926
23	Repatriation of Seamen	1926
24	Sickness Insurance (Industry)	1927
25	Sickness Insurance (Agriculture)	1927
26	Minimum Wage—Fixing Machinery	1928
29	Forced Labor	1930
30	Hours of Work (Commerce and Offices)	1930
52	Holidays with Pay	1936
62	Safety Provisions (Building)	1937
80	Final Articles Revision	1946
81	Labor Inspection	1947
87	Freedom of Association and Protection of the Right to Organize	1948
88	Employment Service	1948
95	Protection of Wages	1949
98	Right to Organize and Collective Bargaining	1949
99	Minimum Wage—Fixing Machinery (Agriculture)	1951
100	Equal Remuneration	1951
101	Holidays with Pay (Agriculture)	1952
104	Abolition of Penal Sanctions (Indigenous Workers)	1955
105	Abolition of Forced Labor	1957
106	Weekly Rest (Commerce and Offices)	1957
107	Indigenous and Tribal Populations	1957
111	Discrimination (Employment and Occupation)	1958
116	Final Articles Revision	1961
129	Labor Inspection (Agriculture)	1969
137	Dock Work	1974

Source: ILO, *Chart of Ratification of International Labour Conventions* (Geneva: International Labour Office, 1981).

to assist in the resolution of labor disputes and who are also empowered to supervise compliance with the Labor Code.

Firms are required to submit semi-annual and annual reports to the Ministry of Labor on the following subjects: hours of work and wages; the number, sex, age, and nationality of workers; fringe benefits; work rules; health regulations; severance pay; industrial accidents; transportation subsidies to workers; life insurance; capitalization of the firm; distribution of overalls and shoes; educational subsidies; and contributions to the National Apprenticeship Service (Servicio Nacional de Aprendizaje). Regional labor inspectors evaluate the data submitted by firms in their regions in order to determine whether Labor Code regulations are being followed. These inspectors are permitted to visit plants without notice to verify the truth of data submitted by firms. If violations of the Labor Code are found, fines ranging from 50 to 2,000 pesos may be levied on the firm. In areas where there is no regional labor inspector, village mayors carry out this function.

WAGES, HOURS, AND WORKING CONDITIONS

The working conditions prescribed by the Colombian Labor Code are summarized in Table IV-3, as well as discussed below. The code specifies laws on recruitment, employment conditions, and dismissals.

Hiring

Any enterprise hiring more than ten employees must comply with certain restrictions on the number of foreigners in its work force. At least 80 percent of the managers, skilled workers, and specialists must be Colombian, with the ratio increasing to 90 percent for unskilled workers. Colombian workers performing work similar to that of foreign employees are entitled to request similar remuneration and general working conditions. The Ministry of Labor can grant special authorizations to modify these ratios to acquire necessary technical expertise only for the time needed to adequately train a Colombian.

To facilitate employers' dismissal of workers whose performance does not meet required standards, the code provides for a probation period known as "período de prueba." The probation lasts two months, during which the contract can be terminated unilaterally at any time. The worker is entitled to all the benefits

TABLE IV-3

Summary of Regulations Concerning Wages, Hours, and Working Conditions

Hiring	In any enterprise hiring more than ten employees, at least 90 percent of the regular workers and 80 percent of the managerial or specialized employees must be Colombian. The Ministry of Labor can authorize a reduction in the proportion of Colombians only in cases dealing with technical personnel and only for the time needed to train adequately a national to perform the job. During the first two months of a working contract ("período de prueba"), the employer or the employee can terminate the relationship at will and without previous notice. Dismissed employees are entitled to all benefits due them based on their length of service.
Remuneration	Equal wages must be paid for equal work irrespective of age, sex, nationality, race, religion, political orientation, or union involvement. Employees working on a daily basis ("jornaleros") are paid weekly, while salaried workers must be paid at least once every month. Regular night work (6 P.M. to 6 A.M.) is paid at a 35 percent premium over normal daily wages. Overtime work carries a 25 percent premium. Night overtime carries a 75 percent surcharge. Wages are paid for days of compulsory rest and vacation. Sunday work carries a 200 percent surcharge. The government decrees minimum wages.
Hours	For all workers, with the exception of management, those in positions of trust, domestic workers, and professional drivers, the regular workday may not exceed eight hours, and the regular workweek should not exceed forty-eight. Overtime is permitted to a maximum of twelve hours per week. If overtime work is deemed necessary as part of the regular operation, authorization must be sought from the Ministry of Labor.
Paid Rest	Workers are entitled to paid rest on Sundays and holidays. There are eighteen paid holidays in a year: January 1 and 6, March 19, June 29, July 29, August 7 and 15, October 12, November 1 and 11, and December 8 and 25; in addition, Holy Thursday, Good Friday, Corpus Christi, the Ascension of Our Lord, and Sacred Heart day are paid days off. Employees working on Sunday or any given holiday are entitled to compensatory paid rest or a corresponding payment at will.
Vacations	Every worker is entitled to fifteen days' paid vacation for each year of uninterrupted work. He must use six of the fifteen days every year. The residual can be

TABLE IV-3 (continued)

	accumulated for up to two years or up to four in special cases. Vacations cannot be replaced by compensatory payments. Only when the worker's contract terminates are employers permitted to replace vacations by cash.
Dismissal	Under indefinite-term contracts, employers dismissing without just cause are required to pay an indemnity of at least forty-five days' salary. Employees willing to terminate an indefinite-term contract should give a one-month advance notice in writing. For fixed-term contracts, employers firing without just cause must pay the compensation that would have been paid for the duration of the contract.
Minors and Women	The law prohibits work by minors under age 14 in industrial or extractive enterprises. Work in the agricultural sector is permitted if it does not preclude attendance at school. Women and minors under 18 are not permitted to work either at night in industrial enterprises or at any time in underground mines or physically demanding jobs. Pregnant women are entitled to an eight-week paid leave at time of birth. In case of abortion or miscarriage, the time is shortened to between two and four weeks.

Sources: Torres, ed., *Código Sustantivo del Trabajo y Código Procesal del Trabajo*; Charry, "Colombia," in *International Encyclopaedia for Labour Law and Industrial Relations*; U.S. Department of Labor, *Labor Law and Practice in Colombia*, pp. 46-64; Price Waterhouse & Co., *Doing Business in Colombia,* April 1978, pp. 42-50.

accrued in his name during his stay with the company. Once the initial two months are over, dismissal or resignation must follow the guidelines provided in the code.

Employment agencies play a minor role in hiring. The government offers free employment exchanges through the National Employment Service (Servicio Nacional de Empleo) and offices maintained by the National Apprenticeship Program. The prevalent methods of recruiting include spreading word of vacancies, newspaper advertisements, and hiring at the plant gate (especially for nonskilled personnel).

Wages

Equal wages must be paid for equal work irrespective of age, sex, nationality, religion, political orientation, or union involvement.

The code differentiates between day and night work. Day work is considered to be any work done between 6 A.M. and 6 P.M. Regular night work carries a 35 percent premium over regular daily wages. Daily overtime is paid at a 25 percent premium over regular daily work; night overtime carries a 75 percent surcharge over regular daily wages.

Employees working by the day are entitled to seven days' pay for six days' work. If they work on Sunday, they receive double pay for the hours worked. Employees paid on a weekly or monthly basis are entitled to receive compensation for Sunday work at double the ordinary rate. In operations requiring successive night-day-night rotations, employers and workers can determine uniform salaries for both day and night work. These salaries should compensate the legal surcharges incurred by working at night.

The National Wage Council advises the Ministry of Labor and Social Security about the desirable level of minimum salaries. Chaired by the minister of labor or his delegate, the council is composed of the following representatives: one each from the Ministries of Finance, Development, and Agriculture; two from the Ministry of Labor; one from the National Council for Economic Policy and Planning; two from private-sector employers; two from private-sector wage and salary earners; one from public employees; and one from public and private pensioneers.[5] If the council fails to reach an agreement, the government can establish minimum wages by decree. The workers' representatives have traditionally been from the democratic confederations: the Union of Colombian Workers (Unión de Trabajadores de Colombia—UTC) and the Confederation of Colombian Workers (Confederación de Trabajadores de Colombia—CTC).

Some years ago, wages were set for different geographic zones and economic sectors, according to the size of the firm. The process has been repeatedly streamlined, and today only two minimum salaries exist, one for the rural and one for the urban sector. The minimum monthly salary, which sets wages for about one-third of the work force,[6] was set as of January 1, 1982, at 7,020 pesos for the rural sector and 7,410 pesos for the urban sector

---

5 U.S. Department of Labor, *Labor Law and Practice in Colombia*, BLS Report No. 408 (Washington, D.C.: U.S. Government Printing Office, 1972), p. 58.

6 Martha R. Lowenstern, *Country Labor Profile: Colombia* (Washington, D.C.: U.S. Department of Labor, Bureau of International Labor Affairs, 1979), p. 8.

(Col. Ps. 59 = US$1).[7] State employees received an across-the-board increase of 25 percent.

Hours

The regular workday is eight hours, and the regular workweek cannot exceed forty-eight hours. Managers, those in positions of trust, domestic workers, and professional drivers are excluded. Shorter hours may be established by collective contract. Positions authorized for sixteen-year-old minors carry a maximum legal workday of six hours.

The maximum of allowable work hours can be extended under various circumstances. The forty-eight-hour limit can be extended to up to sixty hours by seeking authorization from the Ministry of Labor. The eight-hour limit can be relaxed to allow for additional work to replace the four hours on Saturday afternoon. An eight-hour workday for agricultural workers has recently been instituted by the government.[8] Workdays for watchmen were also reduced from twelve to eight hours per day. Professional drivers have repeatedly tried to obtain normal working schedules, but so far to no avail.

Paid Rest and Vacations

Colombia observes eighteen annual holidays (see Table IV-3). Sunday or holiday work can be substituted for by compensatory paid rest or by a corresponding payment at the worker's discretion. If payment is made, it must include the corresponding holiday premium.

After one year of service an employee is entitled to fifteen consecutive working days of paid vacation. The employer may designate, with at least fifteen days' notice, the period in which vacations may be taken. Workers can accumulate their vacations for up to two years, or up to four for highly specialized and trusted technicians or for foreigners working far from their country of origin. Six of the fifteen allowable days must be used every year. Cash compensation in lieu of vacations is only permitted when the worker's contract terminates or in cases in which the national economy or the industry can be jeopardized by the worker's absence.

---

[7] "Colombia Unveils New Minimums," *Business Latin America,* January 20, 1982, p. 19.

[8] Gonzalo Silva Rivas, "Senado aprobó jornada de ocho horas en el campo," *El Espectador,* August 27, 1980, pp. 1-A, 12-A.

Employment Contracts and Dismissal Indemnities

A contract of employment exists, or is presumed to exist, between each employer and employee. Employment contracts need not be written, but the position of an employer is often enhanced by a written contract. Contracts may be for fixed or indefinite terms of employment. A fixed-term contract must always be in writing. The duration cannot be less than one year or more than three, except in the case of temporary labor or other special circumstances. The contract may be renewed indefinitely. A contract of indefinite term remains in effect as long as the activities that caused its origination continue. Both employers and employees are liable under the Labor Code for terminating a contract without just cause. An employee can terminate a contract by paying the employer an indemnity of one month's salary or giving advance written notice of not less than thirty days.[9] Unilateral termination of an indefinite-term contract by an employer without just cause requires payment of a dismissal indemnity amounting to forty-five days' salary when the time of service is not over one year. For continuous service of longer than one year, the employee receives forty-five days' wages for the first year, plus the following additional severance for each year beyond the first:[10]

Years of Service	*Indemnity Payment*
1 to 5	15 days' salary
5 to 10	20 days' salary
10 and beyond	30 days' salary

Under a fixed-term contract, dismissal without just cause requires the employer to pay the compensation that would have been paid for the duration of the contract.

Minors and Women

Colombian labor legislation distinguishes between minors under fourteen, minors under eighteen, and women. Minors under fourteen are prohibited from working in mines, sand and gravel pits, manufacturing, and construction. They are allowed to work in agriculture only if their work does not prevent their attendance at school. Minors under eighteen and women are prohibited from

[9] Price Waterhouse & Co., *Doing Business in Colombia,* April 1978, pp. 45-46; Touche Ross International, *Business Study Colombia,* January 1974, p. 28.

[10] *Ibid.* Amounts are computed on the basis of last monthly salary and for proportion of the year worked.

working at night in jobs that are banned on a regular basis to persons under fourteen. They are also banned from work in underground mines.

The labor law provides for special privileges to pregnant women. At time of birth, women are entitled to an eight-week paid leave. The rest period is shortened to between two and four weeks in the case of abortion or miscarriage.

HEALTH, SAFETY, AND SOCIAL WELFARE

Compensation in Colombia is heavily weighted toward benefits that accrue to the worker and are not directly included in his salary. Manufacturing firms report that fringe benefits add 50 to 65 percent to basic earnings.[11] The Labor Code distinguishes between large and small enterprises on the basis of capital and requires them to provide certain benefits accordingly. Table IV-4 describes the benefits that are common to all employers. Table IV-5 presents those benefits that are applicable only to enterprises having over Col. Ps. 800,000 in capital (US$16,000 as of late 1980).

Social Security

Two organizations are responsible for the administration of social security benefits in Colombia: The National Bureau of Welfare (Caja Nacional de Provisión), which administers the benefits for the public sector, and the Social Security Institute (Instituto de los Seguros Sociales—ISS), which deals with the private sector. The latter was restructured in 1977 in an attempt to improve its level of performance.

Decree 1650 of 1977 stipulates that the mandatory social security benefits provided by the ISS will cover:[12]

—sickness in general
—maternity
—work accidents
—professional sickness
—permanent disability
—old age
—death
—family allowances

---

[11] Lowenstern, *Country Labor Profile*, p. 7.

[12] "Decree Law 1650, July 18, 1977," in Ministry of Labor and Social Security, *Decretos Extraordinarios*, 2nd ed. (Bogotá: Imprenta ISS, 1979), p. 2.

Affiliation with the social security system is mandatory for national and foreign workers, social security functionaries, and pensioneers. Small employers and independent workers can also be affiliated.

TABLE IV-4

Legally Required Benefits

Severance Pay	Workers are entitled to severance pay equal to one month's pay for each year or part thereof of continuous employment with the same firm. Salary at the time of severance is used as the basis for determining severance pay unless the salary has changed during the previous three months, in which case the average salary for the last year of employment is used. Severance pay may be advanced only in the case of a worker who takes leave for military duty or in the case of a worker who wishes to purchase a house or improve his present house. Employers are required to pay 12 percent interest on the accumulated severance pay account of each worker; interest payments must be made at the end of the year.
Life Insurance	All enterprises must carry a collective life insurance policy providing for the payment of one month's salary for each year of service. The minimum payment is twelve months' salary, and in the case of death resulting from work accidents or employment-related illness, the minimum payment is twenty-four months' salary.
Service Bonus	Employees of firms whose capital exceeds Col. Ps. 200,000 are entitled to a bonus of one month's salary payable in two parts: one-half in June and one-half in December. Employees of firms whose capital is less than Col. Ps. 200,000 are entitled to a bonus of two weeks' salary payable in two parts.
Other Payments	Companies with capital greater than Col. Ps. 50,000 or which employ at least ten workers must contribute 6 percent of their payroll to the Caja de Compensación Familiar (Family Compensation Fund). Of this 6 percent, 4 percent goes to family subsidies and 2 percent goes to the national training institute (Servicio Nacional de Aprendizaje).
Shoes and Overalls	Employers must provide blue-collar workers with a pair of shoes and a pair of overalls every four months.
Funeral Expenses	Employers are required to pay funeral expenses of their workers up to a sum equivalent to one month's salary.

Sources: Torres, ed., *Código Sustantivo del Trabajo y Código Procesal del Trabajo*; Charry, "Colombia," in *International Encyclopaedia for Labour Law and Industrial Relations*; U.S. Department of Labor, *Labor Law and Practice in Colombia*, pp. 46-67, 73.

The underlying principle of social security regulation is that enterprises will be responsible for providing the necessary benefits until an operating ISS unit is established near the base of operation. Large enterprises are responsible for the benefits detailed in Table IV-5, while smaller organizations are exempt.

TABLE IV-5
Special Benefits

Pensions	In general, male workers with twenty years of continuous service with the same firm are entitled to receive a pension at age 55. For women, the retirement age is 50. The amount of the pension is normally equivalent to 75 percent of the worker's average earnings during his last full year of employment. The government has the authority to adjust all pensions every time the minimum wage is raised.
	In the government social security system, the retirement age is 60 for men and 55 for women. In order to be eligible for social security benefits, workers must have paid in a minimum of 500 weekly contributions during the twenty years immediately preceding their retirement, or a total of 1,000 weekly contributions in the course of their working life.
Aid for Nonoccupational Injury	If as a result of nonoccupational injury the worker is unable to earn at least one-third of his current income, he is entitled to a compensatory payment according to the seriousness of the injury. Payments vary from one month's salary to a disability pension for up to 30 months' salary (art. 278).
	If the worker is over age 55 and has been with the company for more than fifteen years, his disability pension will be converted into an old-age pension.
Schools and Technical Specialization	Enterprises must furnish a primary school for the children of their workers whenever their plants are at least two kilometers away from any town and there are at least twenty children to be educated.
	Enterprises must provide and maintain one reading school ("escuela de alfabetización") for every forty children of their workers.
	For each 500 workers employed by a firm, and for each additional fraction of 500 above 250, companies must pay for the technical training of one worker or one worker's child. Since the workers themselves have access to the training programs of the Sistema Nacional de Aprendizaje system, these scholarships are usually awarded to workers' children.

Sources: Torres, ed., *Código Sustantivo del Trabajo y Código Procesal del Trabajo*; Charry, "Colombia," in *International Encyclopaedia for Labour Law and Industrial Relations*; U.S. Department of Labor, *Labor Law and Practice in Colombia*, pp. 61, 70.

The company-ISS duality has created an important conflict with respect to pensions. In 1967, the ISS began receiving contributions from employers and employees for the purpose of gradually assuming responsibility for old age and permanent disability pensions. The ISS and the private sector, however, differ in their pension accrual systems. Company pensions are computed at a rate of 75 percent of the average monthly salary earned during the last year and become vested after twenty years of service or at age 55 for men and age 50 for women. The ISS, on the other hand, computes pensions on lower scales and extends the legal age limit five years for both men and women. This means that companies with over Col. Ps. 800,000 in capital will have to carry the burden of the gap between the different pension-computing bases, even once the ISS assumes full responsibility.

An even more serious problem arises from the government's failure to fund ISS programs. Some social security programs in Colombia are financed by employer, employee, and government contributions. The government has failed to fund many of the ISS programs, and the system is crumbling despite desperate reorganization attempts such as the one undertaken by López Michelsen.

Other Entities

Colombia is a leader in the creation of entities to meet workers' needs. This is an indirect means of compensating for low wages. Companies must contribute percentages of their payroll to finance these institutions.

The National Apprenticeship Service, which was created to train workers and provide industry with needed technicians, is a case in point. The Cajas de Compensación Familiar are regionally based institutions that provide pediatric services, discount groceries, and affordable recreation to their affiliates. Similarly, the Family Welfare Institute (Instituto Colombiano de Bienestar Familiar) provides day-care centers and other family-oriented services to aid working parents.

LABOR RELATIONS

Legislation concerning collective labor disputes and their resolution dates from 1919. The first law concerning trade unions was Act 83 of June 23, 1931, which is based on Article 44 of the constitution. This article provides that all persons are permitted "to form companies, associations and foundations that are not contrary to the morals or to legal order. Associations and foundations may obtain recognition as judicial persons."[13] Provisions stipulating the requirements for union formation and membership, as well as the process for resolving labor disputes, were incorporated into the Labor Code in 1950 and then modified or amplified by Decrees 2351 of 1965, 939 of 1966, and Act 48 of 1968. More recently, Decree 1469 of 1978 introduced regulation pertaining to union organization and membership. Table IV-6 highlights the main aspects of collective labor relations in Colombia.

TABLE IV-6

Summary of Collective Labor Relations Law

Organization	Enterprise, craft, industrial, and mixed unions are formally recognized in the code. Only one enterprise union may exist in any undertaking; if more than one exists, the one with the largest membership will prevail. Twenty-five members are required to form a union. Five members is the minimum for an employers' association. Any local or regional federation must have a minimum of ten affiliated unions for legal recognition. For national federations, the minimum is raised to twenty. Confederations must have at least ten affiliated federations. Workers' organizations must be registered with the Ministry of Labor. A union or confederation may legally operate if it has received official recognition ("personería jurídica").
Representation	If in any given undertaking an enterprise union coexists with a craft or industrial one, the one affiliating the majority of the workers will be the workers' representative. If none hold a majority, representation will be shared.
Age and Nationality Requirements	Union members must be over age 14. Two-thirds of the members of any union must be Colombian for it to gain official recognition. Foreigners are not eligible for the position of union director at any level.
Union Protection Rights ("fuero sindical")	Union organizers are protected from dismissal, transfer, or demotion from the date that they notify a competent authority of their intention to sixty days after official publication of that notice, or a total period of not more than six months.

[13] OAS, *Constitution of the Republic of Colombia 1886,* Article 44.

TABLE IV-6 (continued)

	Principals and substitutes on the union board are protected during their term in office and up to six months after its conclusion. The same provision applies to members of the statutory claims commission.
Right to Strike	All workers are entitled to strike except those working in "public utilities, services, or government." Article 430 of the Labor Code establishes which activities are grouped as public services.
Collective Bargaining	With the exception of public employees, all workers are entitled to engage in collective bargaining. Collective agreements signed between employers and unions representing less than one-third of the workers are only applicable to union members and to those that join after the agreement. Agreements signed with unions representing over one-third of the work force are applicable to all workers. If collective agreements have been signed by over two-thirds of the workers in a given industry in a given region, the government is entitled to extend it, in whole or in part, to other enterprises in that industry in the same region. If the duration of the collective agreement is not appropriately stipulated in its text, it is assumed to be validated for successive six-month periods, unless it is opportunely denounced. Collective agreements generally last for two years. The Labor Code also recognizes agreements between nonunionized workers and employers (collective pacts) and union contracts signed between employer(s) and union(s) for the rendering of services by the union members.
Labor Disputes	Whenever a labor dispute arises that could eventually lead to a work disruption or compulsory arbitration, workers must select a committee to present the list of demands to their employer. Dialogue between workers and the employer must start within five days after the demands are presented. Direct conversations may last fifteen days, with an allowable extension of up to ten days. If no agreement is reached during the direct conversation stage, the two parties must elect one conciliator, or one each if they so wish. The employer must name three representatives to act on its behalf during the conciliation stage. The workers' representatives are those that presented the demands. The conciliation stage should last no more than fifteen days. A ten-day extension can be obtained if both parties so consent.

TABLE IV-6 (continued)

	If no settlement is reached after the conciliation stage, the general workers' assembly must decide whether to go on strike or convoke an arbitration tribunal. If a strike is called, the work stoppage may not begin for five days and cannot last more than thirty days. When a strike lasts over ten days, the government may create a tripartite tribunal to propose solutions to the conflict. The workers must vote on the proposals. If no effective results are obtained, the process can be repeated every twenty days. A tripartite tribunal convened to resolve a labor dispute should pronounce its decision within ten days of its formation. The tribunal's decision is binding and lasts for up to two years. Compulsory arbitration applies to all conflicts in the public services.

Sources: Torres, ed., *Código Sustantivo del Trabajo y Código Procesal del Trabajo*; U.S. Department of Labor, *Labor Law and Practice in Colombia*, pp. 31-33, 38-44.

Organization

Four different types of unions are officially recognized in Article 356 of the Labor Code:

1. enterprise ("de base")—composed of members of various professions or occupations in the same undertaking;
2. industrial ("de industria")—including persons employed in firms in the same industry;
3. craft ("gremiales")—consisting of employees in the same occupation or trade; and
4. mixed ("de oficios varios")—consisting of workers of different occupations.

The last type of organization is permitted only when there are not enough workers of similar occupation to form a craft union at any given place. To gain official recognition, unions must meet the requirements presented in Table IV-6, plus others of a more specific nature that are listed in Article 364 of the Labor Code.

Decree 1469 of 1978 introduced minimum requirements for the creation of regional or national federations and also of confederations. Existing organizations that did not meet the requirements were allowed to continue. This decree went further to grant automatic official recognition to unions that fail to receive notification from the Ministry of Labor within fifteen days after filing the required documents. Decree 1469 also states that federations and confederations are permitted to offer advice to their affiliates in individual or collective negotiations.

The enterprise union has historically been the main representative of Colombian workers; only in the past two decades has the government granted special recognition to alternate forms of organizations. At present, unions holding a majority of the work force, irrespective of their organizational nature, are entitled to represent workers' interests in the negotiation of collective contracts.

Collective Bargaining

The Labor Code distinguishes between three types of collective contracts: collective agreements ("convenciones colectivas"), agreements concluded between employers and unions; collective covenants ("pactos colectivos"), agreements concluded between employers and nonunionized workers; and trade union contracts ("contratos sindicales"), agreements between employers and a union for the hire of services or the execution of a particular job rather than for a specified length of time.

Colombian legislation has generally promoted collective bargaining as a means of fostering union affiliation. The right to representation in collective bargaining is guaranteed to all workers except public-sector "employees," one of two groupings of workers in the public sector. The other public-sector grouping, "official workers," may sign collective agreements. The basic principles underlying Colombian collective bargaining are presented in Table IV-6.

In keeping with its generally pro-union stance, the Colombian government has tried to de-emphasize collective covenants and to promote the use of collective agreements. As of 1978, companies are prohibited from signing collective covenants with nonunion employees if a collective agreement with unions representing at least one-third of the work force is in force.

As indicated in Table IV-6, if a collective agreement is signed by a union representing more than one-third of the workers in a given facility, the terms of the agreement are applicable to all workers in that facility. Nonunion workers who benefit from such an extension of the contract are required to pay the union an amount equal to ordinary union dues, unless they specifically renounce the benefits that would accrue to them under the contract. In practice, however, such payments are usually collected only by the stronger unions.

Collective bargaining procedures are clearly defined in the Labor Code, and the employer has an obligation to bargain with employees (whether union or nonunion) if they have followed the prescribed procedures. Colombian labor unions have frequently relied on the intervention of government officials at an early stage in the bargaining process to obtain more favorable settlements than they could obtain through direct negotiation with employers.

Labor Disputes

Disputes arising from economic causes or from conflict of interests are dealt with in the manner described in Table IV-6, which summarizes the relevant legislation. Depending on the circumstances, a dispute can be reconciled through the stages of direct settlement, conciliation, or strike or arbitration. Disputes over very specific issues, such as failure to honor particular clauses of a legal contract, are settled in the labor courts.

Labor courts are a necessary complement to any collective bargaining system, and in Colombia the labor courts fulfill a variety of functions:[14]

> In general terms, and in accordance with Article 2 of the Code of Labour Procedure, the jurisdiction of the labour courts is established for the settlement of legal disputes which arise directly or indirectly from employment contracts. It is also concerned with the fulfilment of the obligations concerning working relations; with the legal rights of organized labour; with authorizations to dismiss pregnant workers; with the dissolution and liquidation of professional associations or unions; with the disputes, actions and remedies provided by the legislation on social security and appeals against the awards of arbitrators. At one time it was also concerned with the question of strikes, the granting of permits to those who are under age with regard to certain activities, and with the revocation of the legal personality of unions. Currently these functions are fulfilled by the Ministry of Labour, except for those relating to workers under eighteen years of age, since they no longer require authorization to carry out certain activities, as that granted to enter into a contract is sufficient.

Prior to 1934, there was no separate legal system designed especially for labor matters; labor cases were heard in the civil court system. In 1934 a separate area of labor jurisdiction was

---

[14] Guillermo González Charry, "Colombia," in R. Blanpain, ed., *International Encyclopaedia for Labour Law and Industrial Relations*, Vol. 2 (The Netherlands: Kluwer, 1979), p. 120.

established, still, however, under the general jurisdiction of the civil courts. Legislative Act 1 of 1940 provided for the creation of a separate labor judiciary, initially structured along the same lines as the civil system. In 1945 the system of local and regional labor courts of appeal was established. For a number of years the labor courts were autonomous, but in 1957 the Supreme Labor Court was abolished as an independent body and became the Labor Division of the Supreme Court of Justice. Regional labor courts were merged into district superior courts, and the local labor courts continued to deal exclusively with labor matters but were incorporated into the circuit court system.

The Labor Code includes a detailed description of the steps that must be followed in settling labor disputes. The first step is a direct meeting between a three-member committee of workers and a representative of management in which the workers present a statement outlining their demands. This stage is known as the "direct agreement" phase, or "arreglo directo." If no agreement can be reached in the first phase, the parties to the dispute must submit to mandatory conciliation by a person acceptable to both parties or, if no one can be found who is acceptable to both parties, by two conciliators designated by each party to the dispute. If the conciliator is unable to bring the parties together, the Ministry of Labor must be notified and the parties must choose between arbitration by the Ministry of Labor and a strike (or lockout).

The Right to Strike

The constitution guarantees all Colombian workers except those in public service the right to strike. The government can define a given industry as a public-service industry if it serves basic public needs or if a work stoppage in that industry would significantly affect the national interest. The Labor Code currently defines the following industries as public service industries:

1. All branches of government service.
2. Transportation, communications, and public utilities.
3. Hospitals, clinics, and other health care facilities.
4. Milk stations, slaughterhouses, and enterprises involved in the distribution of food.
5. Sanitation and garbage collection agencies.
6. Entities involved in the mining, processing, and distribution of salt.

7. Charitable organizations and organizations providing social services.
8. Entities involved in the mining, refining, transportation, and distribution of fuels.
9. Banks.

In addition to these restrictions on the right of workers in certain industries to strike, strikes may be declared illegal by the government if they meet one or more of the following conditions:

1. They pursue goals which are clearly not of a professional or economic nature.
2. They are declared before the stipulated means of dispute resolution (direct agreement, conciliation) are completed.
3. They are declared by vote of a nonrepresentative group of workers.
4. They are declared more than two months after the completion of the conciliation stage.
5. They are not restricted to a peaceful suspension of work.
6. They are intended to pressure the government into performing an action which is reserved to the decision of the government.

If a strike is declared illegal, employers may dismiss all participants, even those protected under the union protection right ("fuero sindical"). Legal recognition of the striking union may also be withdrawn for periods ranging between two and six months. Unions that strike in industries defined as public-service industries may have their official recognition ("personería jurídica") rescinded indefinitely.

CHAPTER V

Organized Labor in Colombia

About 20 percent of the total Colombian work force is organized into labor unions. The urban work force is about 35 percent organized, while in the rural areas only 10 percent of the work force belongs to unions.[1] There are four major nationwide labor confederations, whose combined membership is estimated at between 1,040,000 and 1,340,000.[2] An additional 200,000 workers belong to about 400 independent unions, bringing the total number of unionized workers in the country to between 1,200,000 and 1,500,000.

The level of unionization varies widely by industry. The most heavily unionized industries in the manufacturing sector are steel, textiles, and beverages. Transportation and communication workers are highly organized, as are employees of banking and insurance firms. White-collar workers in the public sector are also heavily unionized.

HISTORICAL OVERVIEW

The origins of organized labor in Colombia can be traced to the nineteenth century, but despite its fairly long history, the labor movement remains divided and weak. The two largest confederations in the country grew under the protection of governments, usually Liberal, which gained popular support by enacting pro-labor legislation.

Origins

The first important workers' organization in Colombia was the Sociedad de Artesanos de Bogotá, created in 1847 by artisans in Bogotá for the purpose of preventing European competition from

---

[1] Martha R. Lowenstern, *Country Labor Profile: Colombia* (Washington, D.C.: U.S. Department of Labor, Bureau of International Affairs, 1979), p. 3.

[2] See Table V-4.

entering the country. Eventually, the artisans' group became more politically oriented and changed its name to Sociedad Democrática. The group was active in Liberal politics for several years but declined in importance in the 1860s. Rival groups sponsored by the Conservatives also emerged during this period, but neither the Liberal nor the Conservative groups were labor unions in the modern sense.

During the second half of the nineteenth century, Colombia suffered several civil wars. These were years of permanent unrest and no important workers' organizations emerged, although many mutual-aid associations were established.[3] During this period, Colombia became a large exporter of coffee, and although the influx of foreign currency spurred industralization in some areas, the economy was still overwhelmingly agricultural. The growth of the organized labor movement was therefore very slow.

In the first two decades of the twentieth century, the Catholic Church established workers' organizations, but these were mostly created for religious purposes. In general, the workers' movement remained weak, since few labor groups received official recognition from the government. At this time, civil law guidelines were applied to the formation of workers' organizations and to the resolution of labor disputes.[4]

Marxist Domination (1920-1930)

In January 1918, the longshoremen of Barranquilla organized the first important strike in Colombia. They petitioned for and, with some difficulty, obtained a 50 percent salary increase. Their example was followed by stevedores in Barranquilla and Santa Marta, the latter joined in their protest by railway men.[5] It did not take long for the wave of strikes that started in the coastal cities to spread across the country: United Fruit Company employees presented a series of demands in 1918; railroad workers went on strike in Medellín and Bogotá; and salary increases were demanded by employees of industries in Bogotá.[6]

---

[3] Miguel Urrutia Montoya, *Historia del Sindicalismo en Colombia* (Medellín: Editorial La Carreta, 1976), pp. 28-29.

[4] Victor Manuel Moncayo and Fernando Rojas, *Luchas Obreras y Política Laboral en Colombia* (Bogotá: Editorial La Carreta, 1978), p. 36.

[5] Urrutia Montoya, *Historia del Sindicalismo*, p. 80.

[6] Moncayo and Rojas, *Luchas Obreras*, p. 38.

Despite the widespread wave of protests, the workers' movement lacked organization. In an attempt to capitalize on the popular unrest, the socialists organized, by year-end 1918, the Confederation of Social Action (Confederación de Acción Social—CAS), which eventually became a new political party. Under the tutelage of the CAS, the Sindicato Central Obrero sponsored the first workers' congress in 1919, at which a platform stressing the labor movement's independence from traditional partisan politics and its commitment to socialist principles was approved. As a result of this congress, many of the mutual-aid associations evolved into trade unions, and many became actively involved in the labor movement. Between 1918 and 1920, many strikes were called by tailors, cobblers, and construction workers in different cities.

With a strengthened workers' movement increasingly involved in work stoppages, the government was compelled to regulate labor disputes, which had been previously dealt with under civil law. In Act 78 of 1919 the government legally acknowledged the right to strike for better salaries and working conditions. This act was later complemented by Act 21 of 1920, under which workers were required to inform their employers of their demands in order to seek a direct agreement before a strike could be called. This act also banned strikes by public-service employees, including those in enterprises providing transportation by land or water, basic utilities, and national mines. In addition to creating a legal framework for labor disputes, the government developed its administrative structure: Law 83 of 1931 established the General Work Office to deal directly with labor matters.[7]

The socialists were unable to retain their grip on the workers' movement for very long. During the second workers' congress, convoked by the Sindicato Central Obrero in 1924, the communists seized control of Colombian labor. Throughout the 1920s, they were successful in staging very important strikes but failed to organize a real mass movement.

The communists oriented their efforts toward disrupting the operations of North American companies in Colombia, which operated under extremely poor industrial relations policies that facilitated the indoctrination of their employees. Seriously disruptive strikes were called in 1924 and 1927 against the Tropical Oil Company in support of a demand for better salaries and working conditions. The company delayed negotiations and finally

[7] *Ibid.*, p. 45.

requested government intervention, which was often violent in strike situations.[8]

The strike that was to have the most significant repercussions, however, was the strike against the United Fruit Company, the bloodiest ever in Colombian labor history. At the invitation of the communists, Spanish and Italian anarchists arrived in 1925 to agitate the workers of United Fruit, which operated in the northern department of Magdalena.[9] Poor working conditions and the coupon system of remuneration[10] provided the discontent needed to organize a major strike. In November of 1928, a general strike was called after the company refused to negotiate a set of demands submitted by the employees. The workers asked the company to stop hiring through subcontractors, a system by which it avoided basic employer responsibilities; demanded salary increases and the abolition of the coupon system; and requested the recognition of their union and of their right to collectively bargain.[11] The government sent in the army to help control the situation. When the strike lasted longer than expected, the soldiers clashed with the workers and many were killed. A correspondent of a leading Bogotá newspaper estimated that 100 workers were killed and 228 wounded.[12]

The political implications of the "bananeras massacre," as this incident later came to be known, were twofold. First, the Conservatives damaged the already shaky prestige of their government and opened the road for the first Liberal presidency in the twentieth century. Second, the Liberals were made to realize the importance of the workers' movement and moved to contest communist dominance over Colombian labor. Thus, the Marxist era came to an end; however, the communists would continue to have a very important role in the development of organized labor.

Growth under Liberal Sponsorship (1930-1945)

During his regime (1930-1934), Enrique Olaya Herrera launched the first of a series of Liberal-sponsored reforms that in the subsequent fifteen years would change the labor environment

[8] Urrutia Montoya, *Historia del Sindicalismo*, p. 118.

[9] *Ibid.*, p. 125.

[10] Workers were paid with coupons that were redeemable only in company stores.

[11] Urrutia Montoya, *Historia del Sindicalismo*, pp. 126-27.

[12] *Ibid.*, p. 129.

in Colombia. The 1930 elections persuaded the Liberals that their support was based in the workers and, as Urrutia points out, they decided to cultivate it:

> The liberal party, which won the 1930 election backed by the working sector, had political reasons to be interested in developing a strong and numerous labor movement. Therefore, as soon as it attained power, that party committed itself to the creation of the legal and institutional conditions necessary to develop a massive labor movement incorporating the skilled and semi-skilled workers which constituted its electoral base.[13]

That the Liberals were committed to labor growth is easily verified by the number of unions that gained official recognition between 1930 and 1946 compared to the figures of previous years (see Table V-1).

Legislation favorable to the labor movement promulgated by the Olaya Herrera government included Law 83 of 1931, by which

TABLE V-1
Number of Officially Recognized Workers' Associations, 1909-1965

Year	Number Recognized	Year	Number Recognized	Year	Number Recognized
1909	1	1928	9	1947	48
1910	4	1929	8	1948	102
1911	3	1930	14	1949	112
1912	1	1931	16	1950	59
1913	2	1932	17	1951	41
1914	3	1933	20	1952	40
1915	1	1934	64	1953	43
1916	4	1935	84	1954	60
1917	8	1936	38	1955	68
1918	4	1937	159	1956	86
1919	1	1938	95	1957	129
1920	5	1939	57	1958	157
1921	4	1940	71	1959	244
1922	3	1941	54	1960	329
1923	5	1942	39	1961	180
1924	9	1943	79	1962	244
1925	7	1944	180	1963	251
1926	5	1945	453	1964	163
1927	8	1946	121	1965	195

Source: Miguel Urrutia Montoya, *Historia del Sindicalismo en Colombia* (Medellín: Editorial La Carreta, 1976), p. 76.

[13] *Ibid.*, p. 135 (authors' translation).

workers' organizations—trade, industrial, and mixed—were formally recognized; employers were forced to accept labor groups that had been granted government recognition; unions were allowed to associate in federations and confederations; collective bargaining was officially acknowledged as a union's right; and the establishment of more than one union in any enterprise was forbidden. The act did not grant union leaders protection from dismissal and also defended the right of nonunionized employees to work, thus permiting the use of strikebreakers.[14]

The reforms initiated by Olaya were later consolidated by Alfonso López Pumarejo, who served as president from 1934 to 1938 and from 1943 to 1945. Under his stewardship, government-labor relations improved, the labor movement grew in size and importance, and new regulations were introduced that benefited Colombian workers. Eduardo Santos, a moderate Liberal who ruled between the two López Pumarejo administrations, maintained a neutral position toward labor that neither helped nor hurt the labor movement.

The formation of the first major workers' confederation is the most significant achievement of the first López period. After an unsuccessful attempt in 1935, the Colombian Union Confederation (Confederación Sindical de Colombia—CSC) was finally established in 1936.[15] From the outset, internal strife beset the ranks of the CSC, as communist and Liberal factions clashed. Strong government backing prevented the disintegration of the organization, which in 1943 changed its name to the Confederation of Colombian Workers (Confederación de Trabajadores de Colombia—CTC). The CTC is today the second largest workers' organization in the country.

Many of the social benefits now enjoyed by Colombian workers were enacted during the López era, especially during his second administration, when the ties with labor grew even closer. López owed his reelection to the lower classes and, after popular demonstrations helped defeat a military coup in 1944, he realized that only workers' support would maintain him in office.

Act 6 of 1945 was originated amid favorable government-labor relations and was a means of invigorating the government's image, which had come under attack from the opposition. This

---

[14] Edgar Caicedo, *Historia de las Luchas Sindicales en Colombia* (Bogotá: Fondo Editorial Suramerica, 1977), p. 53.

[15] Robert J. Alexander, *Organized Labor in Latin America* (New York: The Free Press, 1965), pp. 134-35.

law laid the foundation for the future development of the labor movement by recognizing the company union ("sindicato de base") as the legitimate workers' representative in collective negotiations. Only one union could be formed in any organization, and federations were permitted to present demands only in the absence of a company or enterprise union.[16] In this fashion, the government gave priority to company unions over industrial and trade organizations. This orientation would so prevail in future labor legislation that the Colombian labor movement could be described as structured around the enterprise union.[17] Act 6 also extended the definition of public service to include milk stations, markets and food distribution establishments, and state-owned slaughterhouses.[18]

The labor movement owed its growth in the period 1930-1945 to close collaboration with the government. Beginning in 1946, when the Conservative Party returned to power, the relationship between labor and the government shifted from one of collaboration to confrontation.

A New Kind of Trade Unionism Emerges (1946-1957)

The division within the Liberal Party during the elections of 1946 (described in Chapter II) led to the election of the Conservative candidate, Mariano Ospina Perez, to the presidency. The CTC had supported the populist Liberal candidate, Jorge Eliecer Gaitán, and vigorously opposed the election of Ospina. Internal divisions within the CTC prevented its opposition to the Ospina government from being effective, however; a general strike called by the CTC in 1947 was a complete failure.[19] The assassination of Gaitán in 1948 prompted the CTC to call another general strike, which would be the last important CTC demonstration for many years. The violence that resulted from the assassination of Gaitán led the Ospina government to close congress and to declare a state of siege, which has been in force since then. The state of siege empowers the government to rule by decree, and the enactment of decrees hampering union growth weakened the CTC. Between 1948 and 1957, the CTC held only one con-

---

16 Urrutia Montoya, *Historia del Sindicalismo*, pp. 173-174; Moncayo and Rojas, *Luchas Obreras*, p. 72.

17 Urrutia Montoya, *Historia del Sindicalismo*, p. 175.

18 Moncayo and Rojas, *Luchas Obreras*, p. 73.

19 Urrutia Montoya, *Historia del Sindicalismo*, p. 208.

gress, and its membership declined from 474 affiliated unions in 1947[20] to 27 affiliated unions in 1957.[21]

The decline of the CTC's influence created an opportunity for the Catholic Church to expand its workers' organizations (which had previously been primarily mutual-aid societies) and to consolidate them into a national confederation rivalling the CTC. In 1946, the Catholic groups founded the Colombian Workers' Union (Unión de Trabajadores de Colombia—UTC), which from its inception declared its independence from partisan politics. This stance was very attractive to workers who had become disenchanted with the political feuds within the CTC and who were more interested in economic gains than in political activism. Large numbers of individual unions disaffiliated from the CTC and reaffiliated with the UTC, which received official government recognition as a national confederation in 1949. By 1957, the UTC had become the largest labor confederation in Colombia.

Neither the Ospina government nor its Conservative successor, the Laureano Gómez government, was able to control the violence which resulted from the assassination of Jorge Eliecer Gaitán. The Gómez government was toppled by a military coup in 1953, and General Gustavo Rojas Pinilla became president. Rojas Pinilla attempted to increase his popular support by forming a new national labor confederation, the National Workers' Confederation (Confederación Nacional de Trabajadores—CNT), which would be loyal to him personally. After some initial successes, the CNT faced strong opposition from the Catholic UTC and declined in importance.

In general, the period 1946-1957 was not favorable to the Colombian labor movement. When Rojas Pinilla was removed by the military in 1957, the provisional military government rescinded many of the antilabor decrees enacted by Ospina, Gómez, and Rojas Pinilla, and placed the labor movement in a position to benefit from the political stability that would come during the National Front governments.

The National Front (1958-1974)

The labor movement responded to the end of the Rojas Pinilla dictatorship and the establishment of the National Front by entering a growth phase that was particularly strong during the

---

[20] Caicedo, *Historia de las Luchas Sindicales*, p. 211.

[21] Urrutia Montoya, *Historia del Sindicalismo*, p. 211.

early 1960s. Both the CTC and the UTC grew in membership and acquired new affiliated unions. In addition, two new national confederations and a large number of independent federations emerged. Almost one-third of the unions existing in 1974 were founded between 1957 and 1962, and the number of independent federations increased from ten in 1957 to twenty-five in 1962.[22] The Rojas-sponsored CNT disappeared as a major confederation. Table V-2 shows the rapid growth of the labor movement under the National Front.

TABLE V-2
Unions Affiliated to Major Confederations

Confederation	Number of Affiliated Unions: Under Rojas Pinilla	1959
UTC	288	580
CTC	27	400
CNT	35	0

Source: Edgar Caicedo, *Historia de las Luchas Sindicales en Colombia,* (Bogotá: Fondo Editorial Suramerica, 1977), pp. 79, 84.

As the CTC recovered its strength, its internal rifts reappeared. A confrontation in 1960 between the communists and the Liberals ultimately led to the disaffiliation of the leftist unions from the CTC. The leftist group, originally known as the Comité de Unidad de Acción y Solidaridad Sindical (CUASS),[23] eventually became the Syndicalist Workers' Confederation of Colombia (Confederación Sindical de Trabajadores de Colombia—CSTC), which was formally established in 1964 as the first communist confederation in Colombia. The CSTC was extremely active during the 1960s, although it did not gain official recognition from the government until 1974. The CSTC rapidly became the third largest confederation in Colombia, as well as the most radical of the major workers' organizations.

The creation of the CSTC had important repercussions. Because it was not aligned with either of the traditional political parties, it was a natural haven for any union opposing the National Front. And because it owes its power to its membership and not to the political establishment, the organization is able to

[22] Moncayo and Rojas, *Luchas Obreras,* p. 196.

[23] Caicedo, *Historia de las Luchas Sindicales,* p. 91.

take radical stands without fear of political consequences. The CSTC espouses class struggle and confrontation, with the strike as its favorite tool. By providing a forum for the expression of workers' discontent, it introduced a new form of competition to both the UTC and the CTC. The traditional confederations were forced to become more aggressive and more responsive to the needs of their members in order to avoid loss of influence.

The radicalizing influence of the CSTC can be seen in the increasing frequency of strikes during the early and mid-1960s, as presented in Table V-3. In 1965, the UTC formally abandoned its previous policy of political neutrality; its leader, Tulio Cuevas, stated that the UTC would now "demand from the ruling class legislation for all and not only for a privileged group. . . . The UTC has agreed that the new stage, the big boost for the workers' movement would be to become a great political power." [24] Public-sector employees also engaged in frequent strikes, despite the formal prohibition on strikes by government workers. General strikes were called in 1969 and in 1971, and although neither strike was completely successful, they demonstrated a unity among the major confederations that had hitherto been lacking.

TABLE V-3
Strikes in the 1960s

Year	Strikes	Workers Involved
1962	36	48,000
1963	69	110,000
1964	75	118,000
1965	84	171,000
1966	73	100,500
1967	45	n.a.
1968	44	40,881
1969	59	58,000
1970	63	142,000

Source: Caicedo, *Historia de las Luchas Sindicales,* p. 121.
n.a. = not available.

A new national confederation was founded in 1971 by dissidents from the UTC. This organization, which is social-Christian in its orientation, was called the General Confederation of Workers (Confederación General de Trabajadores—CGT). The CGT was formally recognized by the government in 1975 and is the smallest of the four national confederations.

[24] *Ibid.,* p. 107.

RECENT DEVELOPMENTS

Alfonso López Michelsen became president in 1974 and set out to change the labor environment in the country. Less than a month after his inauguration the CSTC was officially recognized. The number of collective agreements and collective covenants signed during the first twenty months of his administration reppresented almost 75 percent of the total signed during the four years of the Pastrana government. The honeymoon between López and labor was short-lived, however. Deteriorating economic conditions and López's failure to deliver many of his promised reforms soon placed labor and government on different sides of the fence.

State employees were the first to clash with the government. During the second half of 1976, medical workers of the Social Security Institute went on strike to protest government efforts to categorize them as public-service employees.[25] After an extended and widely discussed strike, the government agreed to suspend any repressive measure taken in the wake of the strike and promised to restructure the whole social security system.

The social security strike marked the end of López's efforts to work with Colombian labor. His ideas of a concerted economy, a productivity-based salary, and the modifications to the Labor Code previously presented to congress had to be shelved once his labor minister, María Helena de Crovo, resigned under the pressures of the social security strike. The general strike called for September 14, 1977, by the four major confederations (UTC, CTC, CSTC, and CGT) was the lowest point in recent government-labor relations. Even though this strike can be more adequately characterized as a political rather than a labor event, it nevertheless illustrated to Colombian workers the importance of presenting a united front to stage common protests. The September 1977 strike laid the foundation for the creation of the National Union Council (Consejo Nacional Sindical—CNS), which would become the ongoing coordinator of activities among the different confederations.

The National Union Council represents the first attempt by Colombian unions to forget their political and strategic differences and work together for their common benefit. The CNS was intended to begin a new stage in Colombian labor history but so

---

[25] See Juan de Onis, "Doctors strike just one of the crises facing Colombian chief," *The New York Times*, October 20, 1976.

far has failed to carry out its plans. Despite several government attempts to disband it, the CNS remains the only visible link between the major workers' confederations.

According to the CNS's statement of principles, the council is the steering body of any unified action undertaken by the working class or by Colombian workers in general. A tripartite (government, employers, and workers) advisory body, it claims to defend workers' rights and be independent of any political or religious doctrine. Perhaps the principle of greatest significance is the one calling on the different confederations to act on a unified basis in any entity in which they represent workers.[26] If observed, this principle could become a very important tool for strengthening organized labor.

In June 1978, the presidents of the CSTC and the CGT joined their UTC-CTC counterparts as representatives before the ILO for the first time. In addition, representatives of the radical confederations have been given seats on the Social Security Board.[27] Differences still persist, however, with respect to the National Wage Council and other public entities to which only UTC or CTC representatives are admitted.

Perhaps the CNS's greatest achievement to date has been to stimulate alliances between unions of different confederations to foster collective industry agreements. This has worked in the soft drink industry (between UTC and CSTC unions) and in the textile industry (CTC and CSTC unions).

Julio César Turbay replaced Alfonso López as president of Colombia in 1978 and immediately set out to improve government-labor relations. He quickly established dialogue with leaders of the democratic confederations and decreed a minimum salary increase of 33.7 percent, less than the 50 percent requested by workers but more than the 25 percent offered by employers.[28] Turbay also asked the congress for special authorization to develop, through the CNS, a reform of the Labor Code. The council failed to reach agreement with respect to the desired characteristics of the reform during the time authorized by congress. Under these circumstances, the promised reform had to be shelved and will be discussed by future congresses.

---

26 Iván Darío Osorio, "Desarrollo Sindical Colombiano en los Ultimos Doce Años," *Revista Universidad EAFIT*, No. 38, p. 63.

27 Lowenstern, *Country Labor Profile*, p. 4.

28 Richard Booth, *1978 Annual Labor Report* (unclassified document released by American Embassy, Bogotá, March 5, 1979), p. 8.

Turbay's conflicts with labor originated not from his failure to deliver on his pledges of changes in labor regulation but from his reluctance to adjust minimum wages to cost-of-living increases. In its effort to reduce inflationary expectations, the government has allowed real wages to decline. Labor representatives in the National Wage Council held back their approval of the 26.5 percent increase in rural and urban wages enacted in January 1981.[29] Followers of Colombian developments foresee increasingly difficult labor negotiations for firms given the gap that has developed between labor expectations and government and employer offerings with respect to economic issues in labor contracts.[30]

THE MAJOR CONFEDERATIONS AND INDEPENDENT ORGANIZATIONS

The four major Colombian confederations are the UTC, CTC, CSTC, and CGT. The first two are the oldest and are generally acknowledged to be the democratic unions (i.e., those with which the government negotiates labor matters). The CSTC is a communist (pro-Moscow) organization; the CGT, the smallest and most recently formed, is a radical organization of social-Christian orientation.

Both the UTC and the CTC are affiliated internationally to the International Confederation of Free Trade Unions (ICFTU) and regionally to the Interamerican Regional Organization of Workers (Organización Regional Interamericana de los Trabajadores—ORIT). The CSTC is affiliated to the World Federation of Trade Unions (WFTU) and regionally is affiliated to the Congress for Latin American Trade Union Unity (Congreso Permanente para la Unidad Sindical de Trabajadores de América Latina—CPUSTAL). Finally, the CGT is regionally affiliated to the Latin American Confederation of Trade Unions (Central Latinoamericana de Trabajadores—CLAT) and internationally to the World Confederation of Labour (WCL).

In membership, the largest confederation is the UTC, followed by the CTC and CSTC as close second and third, with the CGT

---

29 "Labor Balks at Minimums," *Business Latin America,* January 14, 1981, p. 16.

30 "Colombian Inflation is Pushing Up the Ante in Wage Negotiations," *Business Latin America,* December 10, 1980, p. 400.

a distant fourth. Table V-4 presents membership figures obtained from Ministry of Labor data, as well as information about jurisdiction, leadership, and affiliation.

TABLE V-4
Major Labor Confederations in Colombia

Name	Colombian Workers' Union (Unión de Trabajadores de Colombia—UTC)
Address	Calle 10 #7-33 Bogotá, Colombia
Jurisdiction	Membership broadly includes regional federations and industrial federations in metallurgical, textile, postal and telegraph, and hotel trades.
Claimed Membership	1,878,000 (1979)
Estimated Actual Membership	600,000-700,000 (1979)
Local Affiliations	Regional federations: Cundinamarca (UTRACUN) Antioquía (UTRAN) Industrial federations: Metalworkers (UTRAMMICOL) Textile workers (UTRATEXCO) Postal and telegraph workers (SINTRAPOSTAL) Hotel and restaurant workers (HOCAR) Total: 974 affiliates
International Affiliations	Interamerican Regional Organization of Workers (ORIT) International Confederation of Free Trade Unions (ICFTU)
Leadership	Tulio Cuevas, president Victor Acosta, secretary general
Observations	Founded in 1946; legally recognized in 1949. Colombia's largest labor confederation.
Name	Confederation of Colombian Workers (Confederación de Trabajadores de Colombia—CTC)
Address	Calle 16 #14-13 Piso 5 Bogotá, Colombia
Jurisdiction	The membership includes a powerful and wealthy port workers' union. Various regional federations, the sugar workers' union, and metalworkers.

TABLE V-4 (continued)

Claimed Membership	1,500,000 (1979)
Estimated Actual Membership	250,000-300,000 (1979)
Local Affiliations	Most important regional federations: Barranquilla, Cali (FESTRAVAL—including the sugar workers) Cartagena Most significant industrial federations: Railroad workers Port workers Metalworkers Total: 417 affiliates
International Affiliations	ORIT ICFTU
Leadership	Manuel Felipe Hurtado, president Apecidas Alviz Fernandez, secretary general
Observations	Founded in 1933 and legally recognized in 1948. The CTC is Colombia's oldest labor confederation. Membership has declined over the years as unions have split off. Originally linked to the Liberal Party, it now has members of different political orientations.
Name	Syndicalist Workers' Confederation of Colombia (Confederación Sindical de Trabajadores de Colombia—CSTC)
Address	Calle 14 #15-42 Bogotá, Colombia
Jurisdiction	Membership is primarily composed of public employees. Also workers in beer, cement, textile, transport, and metal industries.
Claimed Membership	n.a.
Estimated Actual Membership	200,000-300,000 (1979)
Local Affiliations	Total: 324 affiliates
International Affiliations	Latin American Workers' Permanent Congress for Trade Union Unity (Congreso Permanente para la Unidad Sindical de Trabajadores de America Latina—CPUSTAL) World Federation of Trade Unions (WFTU)
Leadership	Pastor Perez, president Miguel Antonio Caro, vice president Roso Osorio, secretary general

TABLE V-4 (continued)

Observations	The CSTC was formed in 1960 after communist elements were expelled from the CTC. Legal recognition was granted in 1974. Has lost Maoist-oriented membership.
Name	General Confederation of Workers (Confederación General de Trabajadores—CGT)
Address	Calle 17 #10-62 Bogotá, Colombia
Jurisdiction	The CGT has focused its organizing efforts on the "campesinos."
Claimed Membership	n.a.
Estimated Actual Membership	20,400-40,000
Local Affiliations	Total: 123 affiliates
International Affiliations	Confederation of Latin American Workers (Central Latinoamericana de Trabajadores—CLAT) World Confederation of Labour (WCL)
Leadership	Efren Delgado, president Pablo Emilio Pinzon, secretary general
Observations	The CGT is an outgrowth of a Catholic workers' association that broke away from the UTC. The CGT gained legal recognition in 1975.
Name	Independent and Revolutionary Workers' Movement (Movimiento Obrero Independiente Revolucionario—MOIR)
Address	n.a.
Jurisdiction	Mainly composed of independent, single-company unions in various industrial sectors (petroleum, chemicals, tires, metal, manufacturing, etc.), as well as bank workers and teachers.
Claimed Membership	n.a.
Estimated Actual Membership	n.a.
Local Affiliations	n.a.
International Affiliations	Peking-oriented communist tendencies, but no official affiliations.

TABLE V-4 (continued)

Leadership	n.a.
Observations	The MOIR broke from the CSTC in 1975 but has not gained a significant foothold, at least in terms of the 1978 election results, which gave the MOIR only 1 percent of the vote.

Sources: Martha R. Lowenstern, *Country Labor Profile: Colombia* (Washington, D.C.: U.S. Department of Labor, Bureau of International Affairs, 1979), p. 5; International Confederation of Free Trade Unions, *ICFTU Directory, 1980-1981* (Brussels: ICFTU, 1981); materials from the U.S. Department of State and other, confidential materials in authors' possession.
n.a. = not available.

Independent unions are perhaps the fastest-growing group of organizations among organized labor in Colombia. Important state workers' unions are included in this group, such as the Inter-union Committee of State Workers (Comité Intersindical de Trabajadores del Estado—CITE) and the National Federation of State Workers (Federación Nacional de Trabajadores al Servicio del Estado—FENALTRASE).[31] State-owned enterprises such as Telecom, the national telecommunications company, also have independent unions. Perhaps the best known of the independent unions are the Bank Workers' Association (Asociación Colombiana de Empleados Bancarios—ACEB), the Colombian Teachers' Federation (Federación Colombiana de Educadores—FECODE), and the Oil Workers' Union (Unión Sindical Obrera—USO). It is important to note that the ACEB, FECODE, and the USO are all public-service unions (most of FECODE's members are public teachers) and under Marxist influence. The latter two are the strongest nonaffiliated unions.

The FECODE came to the forefront of Colombian news in 1976 when teachers called a general strike to protest López Michelsen's proposal of a new career statute ("estatuto docente"), which was modified during the initial months of Turbay's administration. The FECODE groups about 120,000 of the nation's teachers and is a center of leftist agitation. In 1978, it withdrew from the CSTC "on the grounds that the latter had sold out to the government."[32] It is presently controlled by communists of varying ideologies.

---

[31] James Dunkerley and Chris Whitehouse, *Unity is Strength—Trade Unions in Latin America—A Case for Solidarity* (London: Latin America Bureau, 1980), p. 80.

[32] Booth, *1978 Annual Labor Report,* p. 4.

The USO is a rich and powerful union of 7,000 to 11,000 workers of the state oil company Ecopetrol. It is dominated by a coalition of various types of communists. The last major strike by the USO occurred in 1977 when the union was suspended and the government sent troops to occupy Ecopetrol installations. A threatened strike scheduled for early 1981 was called back after negotiations.

Maoist unions have grouped to form the Independent and Revolutionary Workers' Movement (Movimiento Obrero Independiente y Revolucionario—MOIR). The MOIR controls important, single-company unions in various sectors of industry (petroleum, chemicals, tires, metal manufacturing) in addition to bank workers and some government employees. It also exercises influence over the FECODE and the USO.[33]

Activities of the International Trade Secretariats

Affiliation of Colombian trade unions to the International Trade Secretariats (ITSs) is described in Table V-5. International organizations have largely limited their activities in Colombia to the sponsorship and organization of seminars to educate workers.

The repressive measures taken under the Turbay administration moved various ITSs to voice protest, and occasionally in their publications they denounce the "security statute" enacted in 1978. Despite this, ITSs remain very distant from the everyday activities of Colombian unions.

Structural Problems

From an organizational perspective, the two greatest problems faced by organized labor are the relative weakness of industrial and craft unions compared to the widespread presence of enterprise or company unions and the personal rivalries between union leaders that tend to divide rather than unite the labor movement.

The government is sponsoring the solidification of unions other than enterprise by adopting favorable legislation. The CSTC has been particularly aggressive in promoting new forms of organization. As CSTC President Pastor Perez has stated: "Unions should organize themselves by industrial branches to be able to more effectively confront employers and government. The presentation of identical demands is a way of developing unity and making

[33] *Ibid.*

TABLE V-5
The International Trade Secretariats in Colombia

International Trade Secretariat	Affiliates	Claimed Membership	Activities
International Federation of Building and Woodworkers (IFBWW)	Sindicato de Trabajadores del Departamento Administrativo de Acción Comunal del Distrito Especial de Bogotá (SINTRACODE)	219 (June 1978)	Union movement in the country is characterized as weak; the building workers are, in particular, poorly organized.
			A seminar was held in conjunction with the IUF for trade union education and to promote greater cooperation between the unions, July 3-8, 1978.
International Transport Workers' Federation (ITF)	Asociación Nacional de Empleados de la Flota Mercante Grancolombiano (ANEGRAN)	327 (1976)	Seminars were conducted in Colombia for women transport workers and for Colombian road transport unions, 1975 and 1974, respectively.
	Unión de Marinos Mercantes de Colombia (UNIMAR)	1,000 (1976)	
	Sindicato Nacional de Trabajadores Ferrovarios	5,000 (1976)	A basic trade union seminar was held for rail and dockworkers; also education seminars for union leaders and for ANEGRAN.
	Federación Nacional de Chóferes y Asalariados del Transporte (FENALCHOL)	2,000 (1976)	
	Asociación Colombiano de Auxiliares de Vuelo (ACAV)	325 (1976)	
	Sindicato Nacional de Chóferes de Colombia	600 (1976)	
	Asociación de Chóferes de Colombia (ASOCHOCOL)	600 (1976)	

TABLE V-5 (continued)

International Trade Secretariat	Affiliates	Claimed Membership	Activities
	Federación Nacional de Trabajadores Portuarios de Colombia (FEDEPUERTOS)	2,000 (1976)	
International Union of Food and Allied Workers' Associations (IUF)	Sindicato de Trabajadores de la Fábrica de Grasas y Productos Químicas (GRASCO)	100 (1981)	Held a seminar in conjunction with the IFBWW to promote trade union education and mutual cooperation, Bogotá, July 3-8, 1978.
	Sindicato de Trabajadores de la Industria Hoteleriá y Gastronómica de Colombia (SINTHOGC)	200 (1981)[a]	
	Sindicato Nacional de Trabajadores de Finca S.A.	180 (1981)	
	Sindicato de Trabajadores de Industrias San Jorge S.A.	100 (1981)[a]	
	Sindicato de Trabajadores de Posada Tobon S.A.	100 (1981)[a]	
	Sindicato Nacional de Trabajadores de Purina Colombiano S.A.	268 (1981)[a]	
	Sindicato Nacional de Trabajadores de Bavaria S.A.	3,000 (1981)[a]	
International Metalworkers' Federation (IMF)	Federación de Trabajadores de las Industrias Metalúrgicas Eléctricas y Mecánicas de Colombia (FETRAMECOL)	15,000 (1980)	FETRAMECOL held seminars to improve the wages and working conditions of women and young people in the metal industry, July 1977. Also won the elimination of collective pacts, August 1979. Held basic education semi-
	Unión de Trabajadores Metalúrgicos y Mineros de Colombia (UTRAMMICOL)	45,000 (1980)	

TABLE V-5 (continued)

			nars and one seminar concerning the family subsidy.
International Federation of Commercial, Clerical, Professional and Technical Employees (FIET)[b]	Sindicato Nacional de Trabajadores de la Industria Gastronómica, Hotelería y Similares de Colombia	1,000 (1979)	In 1978, educational seminars were held by IRO-FIET, the Latin American branch of FIET, in Colombia and other Latin American countries. Trade section meetings were held in Bogotá, 1978. Commerce, banking, insurance, and social security trade section seminars were held in 1979 in Colombia and in other member countries.
	Sindicato Nacional de Trabajadores del Instituto Colombiano de Seguros Sociales	6,000 (1979)	
International Federation of Plantation, Agricultural and Allied Workers (IFPAAW)	Federación Agrarian Nacional, Bogotá (FANAL). FANAL withdrew affiliation from the UTC because of a jurisdictional dispute.	12,000 (1976)	Seminar (1973-1974) for local organizations, continuing labor union education. Developmental small cooperatives on communal projects. The second Peasants' Regional Congress of FANAL was held December 18-19, 1976. In conjunction with FESTRACOL, a course for agricultural workers was held February 27-March 6, 1977.
	Federación Sindical de Trabajadores Agrarias de Colombia (FESTRACOL). Affiliated with the CTC.		Participated in a three-year trade union and vocational education program for women. Sponsored an inter-
			national trade union seminar

TABLE V-5 (continued)

International Trade Secretariat	Affiliates	Claimed Membership	Activities
			for rural workers, July 22-August 10, 1979 (FANAL and FESTRACOL participated). From July 19 to August 12, 1979, a seminar was conducted on leadership and organization of rural workers. Also sponsored the Agricultural Trade Union Leaders' International Seminar on Family Planning, March 25-31, 1979.
International Graphical Federation (IGF)	Sindicato de Artes Gráficas (industrial union)	101 (1978)	No activities were reported.
Postal, Telegraph and Telephone International (PTTI)	Federación Colombiana de Trabajadores de Comunicaciones	6,170 (1977)	Strong organizational drive took place and also a movement to merge the small regional telephone unions into one organization, 1974. In 1975, seminars were sponsored to study the "Simón Rodriguez Agreement," an attempted standardization of the Andean countries' labor laws. In 1976, several independent telephone companies in Colombia became part of the municipal public services

TABLE V-5 (continued)

			and FECOLTRACOM lost two affiliates. Seminar on consumer cooperatives was cosponsored by the PTTI and the NVV, a Dutch foundation, April 1979.
Public Services International (PSI)	Sindicato de Empleados del Departamento Administrativo Nacional del Estadística	800 (1964)	
	Sindicato de las Empresas Unidas de Energia Electrica de Bogotá	400 (1968)	
	Sindicato de Empleados Distritales	800 (1968)	

Sources: IFBWW, "Documents from the Secretariat," *15th Congress, Vienna, August 21-24, 1978* (Geneva: IFBWW, 1978); ITF, "Report on Activities, 1974-1976," *32nd Congress, Dublin, July 21-29, 1977* (London: ITF, 1977), pp. 55-67; IUF, "Secretariat Documents," *19th Congress, Munich, May 1981* (Geneva: IUF, 1981); IMF, "Report of the Secretariat," "Reports of Affiliates," *25th World Congress, Washington, D.C., May 24-29, 1981* (Geneva: IMF, 1981); FIET, "Report on Activities, 1976-1979," *19th World Congress, Caracas, Venezuela, November 26-30, 1979* (Geneva: FIET, 1979), pp. 10, 90-91; IFPAAW, "Current Position in Relation to Affiliations," *4th World Congress, Geneva, December 17-18, 1976* (Geneva: IFPAAW, 1976); IGF, *12th Report of Activities, 1976-1978* (Berne, Switzerland: IGF, 1978), p. 59; PTTI, "Activities Report, 1975-1977," *23d World Congress, Washington, D.C., October 16-20, 1978* (Geneva: PTTI, 1978), p. 116; PTTI Inter-American Office, *Latin American Reports, 1974-1976* (Geneva: PTTI, 1976), pp. 9, 27-28; PTTI, *Inter-American Congress, Caracas, 1977* (Geneva: PTTI, 1977), p. 64; *ibid.*, "Colombia: Consumer Cooperatives," *PTTI News*, No. 8 (August 1979), p. 5; PSI, "Report," *20th Congress, New York, October 8-12, 1973* (Middlesex, England: PSI, 1973), p. 15; *Directory of Labor Organizations*, Vol. I, p. 21.

[a] Had not paid dues for 1981 at this time.

[b] The Federación Nacional de Sindicatos Bancarios Colombianos, which in 1976 had 5,000 members, has disaffiliated.

workers aware of the importance of industrial unionism." [34] While the transformation of the labor movement from a company-based concept to an industrial and trade context will take some time, it can be asserted that workers are aware of the limitations the present structure imposes.

Personal feuding among labor leaders has also played its part in fragmenting the labor movement. In 1972, confrontations between José Raquel Mercado (president of the CTC) and federation representatives led to the disaffiliation of the metal workers' federation, the union of Avianca workers, and an oil and chemical workers' federation. During that same year, Hugo Becerra, probably funded by elements in the Liberal Party, challenged Mercado for the CTC's presidency. UTC leader Cuevas used Mercado's precarious political position to influence him to agree to a UTC-CTC unification effort that did not work. The animosity among CTC leaders continued, and a rift was prevented by the unfortunate assassination of José Raquel Mercado by the terrorist M-19 movement in February 1976.[35] Mercado was replaced by Gustavo Diaz, who was removed in 1978 when Manuel Felipe Hurtado became president of the CTC. In 1980, the workers' union of the National Railways (Ferrocarriles Nacionales) withdrew its affiliation from the CTC,[36] costing the CTC its largest affiliate, with about 12,000 members.

The UTC has also had its share of internal struggles. Tulio Cuevas has had to face many challenges but has protected his position by building a very loyal executive committee that continues to support him. Until 1980, Cuevas had managed to maintain a united UTC despite significant internal differences. A visit by Cuevas to imprisoned M-19 terrorists provided the excuse that the more conservative elements were looking for to part from the UTC. In this case, personal animosity is enhanced by political differences. Cuevas is a member of the progressive wing of the Conservative Party, and Alvaro Ramírez, his contender, belongs to the more traditional faction.[37] The end result of the confrontation was that Ramírez disaffiliated the Workers' Union of Cundinamarca (Unión de Trabajadores de Cundinamarca—UTRA-

---

34 Darío Osorio, "Desarrollo Sindical Colombiano," p. 62.

35 Caicedo, *Historia de las Luchas Sindicales*, p. 164.

36 "Ferroviarios se retiran de la CTC," *El Tiempo*, August 17, 1980, p. 1-A.

37 "Colombia: Leading Labour Group Divided," *Latin America Regional Reports, Andean Group*, December 12, 1980, p. 4.

CUN), with 153 unions and 90,000 members, from the UTC. The UTC immediately created another organization, the Workers' Union of Bogotá and Cundinamarca (Unión de Trabajadores de Bogotá y Cundinamarca—UTRABOC) to replace UTRACUN in the important Bogotá area. Again, disputes of an extremely personal nature were believed to have caused the split.

Political Involvement

The relative weakness of most Colombian unions and their financial inability to withstand protracted strikes have led the major confederations to intensify their political involvement in recent years in order to bolster their bargaining power by enlisting the support of government. The degree of government involvement in labor negotiations and disputes, particularly by top-level officials such as the president and the minister of labor, is very high in comparison to other countries at a similar stage of economic development.[38] Even the UTC, which was originally intended to be apolitical and whose original appeal to the workers derived from its concentration on economic issues, is now openly involved in politics. Although the CTC has always had close links with the Liberal Party and the UTC is generally identified in the public mind as allied to the Conservatives, the political orientation of both confederations has been blurred in recent years. Both the UTC and the CTC have affiliates of varying political tendencies.

The communist-dominated CSTC grew out of mostly leftist-oriented unions that disaffiliated from either the UTC or the CTC. In recent years, however, the CSTC is facing the problems caused by the extreme fragmentation of the Colombian left. As the gap between pro-Moscow and pro-Peking followers widens, the differences between unions of each orientation also increase. Several important individual unions have abandoned the CSTC and joined the Maoist MOIR movement.

The failure of the traditional Liberal and Conservative parties to deliver needed social changes may open the way for the formation of a workers' party. The UTC is beginning to sharpen its rhetorical attacks on the two mainstays of Colombian politics.[39] In view of the divisions in the labor movement, however, the no-

---

38 Lowenstern, *Country Labor Profile*, p. 5.

39 "Labor balks at minimum," *Business Latin America*, January 14, 1981, p. 16.

tion of a workers' party seems extremely distant. There is a strong bipartisan tradition in the country that is not easy to overcome. Nor does there seem to be anyone in the present group of federation leaders who might be capable of leading a united political party.

The four major confederations have failed to create a unified labor movement. Efforts in 1972 to consolidate the UTC and the CTC failed after their leadership could not agree on the reforms to the labor calendar that were then under study by the government. Since then, the CNS notwithstanding, efforts to unify the labor movement have been negligible. On the contrary, major confederations are losing important affiliates. Among the independent unions once affiliated to major confederations, the most important are the petroleum workers' union (USO), the national school teachers' confederation (FECODE), and other large public-sector groups.

State Workers

The government employs 7 to 10 percent of the economically active population. Compared to their private-sector counterparts, state workers are undercompensated and have fewer legally recognized labor rights. These two factors explain why state employees have been so active in calling strikes. They also explain why, despite stiff opposition, the government has tried to include as many employees as possible in the public-employee grouping of government workers. In addition, most of the state workers' organizations are white-collar unions that enjoy a relatively high affiliation rate and increasingly are affiliating to independent federations.[40]

State workers are also organized around enterprise unions that face fragmentation problems similar to those confronting the major confederations. There are five major confederations of state employees: FENANSITRAP, independent; FECOLTRAES, affiliated to the CGT; ULTRADEC, of the UTC; FENALEMPO, of the CTC; and FENALTRASE, which groups unions from the four major confederations.[41] Table V-6 presents a list of the major state workers' unions.

---

[40] María Teresa Herrán, "El estado patrón y sus trabajadores," *El Espectador*, December 15, 1980, p. 7-A.

[41] *Ibid.*, p. 13-A.

TABLE V-6
State Workers' Federations

Federation	Number Affiliated Unions	Number National Unions	Number Regional Unions	Number Workers Represented [a]
FENALTRASE-CITE	54	28	26	218,300
FECODE	54	6	48	172,000
ULTRADEC	42	4	38	21,000
FENANSITRAP	25	4	21	18,600
FENALTRACER	21	2	19	14,200
FEDEPUERTOS	7	1	6	11,000
FENALEMPO	12	5	7	8,400
FEDEPETROL	6	3	3	7,300
FECOLTRACOM	4	2	2	3,300
FELCOLTRAES	6	2	4	3,000
FENTRACAL	7	—	7	2,800
Nonconfederated	52	7	45	62,000
Total	290	64	226	749,900

Source: María Teresa Herrán, "El estado patrón y sus trabajadores," *El Espectador*, December 15, 1980, p. 7-A.

[a] The "Number Workers Represented" column shows the total number of workers employed where the unions are based. Actual affiliation averages 48 percent.

In 1976, an interunion committee (Comité Intersindical de Trabajadores Estatales—CITE) was organized. The CITE succeeded in organizing a state workers' strike in 1977 and, in 1978, merged with FENALTRASE.[42] To date, and thanks to this merger, FENALTRASE is the only federation incorporating unions from all major confederations together with some nonaffiliated or independent unions.

Union Financing

Article 379 of the Labor Code bans union involvement in commercial enterprises. Union funding comes from membership fees, government grants, and international organizations.

In her work on Colombia unionism, journalist María Teresa Herrán asked leaders of the different confederations about their funding from international sources. All were reluctant, given the political implications their replies might have, to identify their sources and the amount of aid received. Union leaders stated that

[42] *Ibid.*

international help was received only in the form of technical advice, sponsorship of nonbudgeted educational programs, and invitations to participate in international events.[43] Given the low union affiliation rates in Colombia and the uncertain pattern of payments from affiliates, it is likely that funds are provided to the different unions from the United States, the Soviet Union, and Europe.

Domestic sources of funding are primarily the government and the affiliates themselves. Collection of fees at the enterprise union level is straightforward, since employers are allowed to deduct union fees from the workers' paychecks. At the federation and confederation levels, the situation is more difficult because payments from affiliated unions and federations are sporadic. The only existing mechanism for monitoring the payment of membership fees is the annual convention, in which only paid-up organizations can participate. Pablo Emilio Pinzón, the CGT's finance secretary, estimates that 30 percent of affiliated organizations pay dues: 50 percent pay on a semiannual basis, and 20 percent pay their dues before the annual convention.[44] Convention participation fees provide the other source of federation and confederation funding from affiliates. In 1979, the UTC collected Col. Ps. 808,609 from regular fees and Col. Ps. 1,639,757 from convention fees.[45]

Government funding of union activities comes from two sources. Until 1980, congressmen were allotted a sum of money which they could donate to institutions of their choice. Many congressmen chose to donate their allottment to workers' organizations. In the first ten months of 1980, unions received Col. Ps. 20 million from this source.[46] Since 1981, congressmen have been required to donate these funds to educational and charitable organizations. This reform was enacted in order to discourage corruption and the embezzlement of public funds. In time, however, it can be expected that unions and politicians will learn to work around the new regulation, perhaps by establishing semiautonomous, union-sponsored educational or charitable organizations.

---

[43] María Teresa Herrán, "Otras fuentes de financiación," *El Espectador*, October 21, 1980.

[44] *Ibid.*, "Como se financían las centrales? *El Espectador*, October 20, 1980, p. 5-A.

[45] *Ibid.*, p. 12-A.

[46] *Ibid.*, "Otras fuentes de financiación."

The second source of government funding for unions is the Ministry of Labor. In the first nine months of 1980, the Ministry of Labor granted more than Col. Ps. 43 million to the UTC and the CTC. These funds are granted according to criteria established by the incumbent minister of labor and not according to any continuous, stated policy.[47] This type of financial support from the Ministry of Labor has only been granted to the democratic confederations (CTC and UTC).

STRIKE ACTIVITY

Strike activity in the 1970s was 16 percent higher than in the 1960s. The average number of workers involved in work stoppages increased from 1,937 in the 1960s to 2,670 in the 1970s. The sectors most affected by strikes during the 1970s were manufacturing (267 strikes), education (125 strikes), and services (188 strikes). Workers in the independent federations and independent unions were the most strike-prone in the 1970s, participating in 42.5 percent of all strikes. Of the major confederations, the communist CSTC was the most active in the 1970s; CSTC workers participated in 29.5 percent of all strikes. Workers affiliated with the UTC participated in 16.5 percent of all strikes, while workers affiliated with the CTC participated in 7.5 percent. The much smaller CGT was involved in only 1 percent of all strikes.[48]

Table V-7 presents data on strikes in the 1970s. A study conducted in late 1980 showed that 29 percent of all strikes in 1980 lasted less than two days; 39 percent lasted between two and forty-three days; and 32 percent lasted more than forty-three days. Companies employing more than 200 workers suffered the longest strikes: of those strikes lasting more than forty-three days, over 60 percent took place in larger companies. Strikes in the public sector accounted for 40 percent of all strikes during 1980.[49]

COLLECTIVE AGREEMENTS

The National Association of Industrialists (Asociación Nacional de Industriales—ANDI) regularly surveys Colombian firms to de-

---

[47] *Ibid.*

[48] *Ibid.*, "Somos un país de huelgas?" *El Espectador*, February 9, 1981, p. 10-A.

[49] *Ibid.*, "Otras valvulas de escape," *El Espectador*, February 10, 1981, n.p.

TABLE V-7
Strikes during the 1970s

Year	Number Strikes	Workers	Workdays Lost	Man-Days Lost
1971	37	152,000	825	2,500,000
1972	67	162,000	1,040	3,880,000
1973	53	105,000	1,250	3,150,000
1974	75	82,800	1,360	940,000
1975	109	197,500	2,366	1,700,000
1976	58	117,100	2,647	2,128,720
1977	93[a]	210,200	2,615	4,697,164
1978	68	366,000	2,422	2,088,936
1979	60	90,200	1,450	2,202,400
1980	49	303,380	1,319	1,758,850
Total	669	1,786,180	17,294	25,046,070

Source: María Teresa Herrán, "Somos un país de huelgas?" *El Espectador*, February 9, 1981, p. 10-A.
[a] Does not include the general strike of September 14, 1977.

termine the basic characteristics of collective agreements. The sample of firms used by ANDI includes firms of all sizes, most major industries, and most major manufacturing regions of the country.

In general, most collectively negotiated contracts in Colombia last two years. Table V-8 presents the duration of collective contracts in various industries in 1978. Only in the metalworking industry was there a significant number of contracts for more than two years. About two-thirds of the salary increases negotiated in 1978 were formulated in lump-sum terms, while the remaining one-third was based on percentage of each worker's salary. The average percentage increase in wages was between 20 and 29 percent.[50] Companies that operate under collective contracts tend to hire workers at above the minimum wage.

In addition to wages and working conditions, typical elements of a Colombian collective contract are vacation bonuses, Christmas bonuses, medical-care benefits, educational benefits, death benefits, and benefits for athletic activities. In general, vacation and Christmas bonuses (and sometimes seniority bonuses) are calculated on the basis of daily wages. For example, the most common vacation bonus in 1978 was between ten and fifteen days' wages,

[50] Asociación Nacional de Industriales, *Convenciones Colectivas*, 1978, p. 305.

while Christmas bonuses averaged between twenty-o[illegible] days' pay. Health benefits are usually exp[illegible] centage of the doctor's (or hospit[illegible] [illegible]ompany or as a lump sum that wi[illegible] [illegible]y, above which the worker must pay [illegible] [illegible]ucational benefits, death benefits, and benefits fo[illegible] activities are normally expressed in lump-sum terms. Th[illegible] percentage of companies surveyed by ANDI that provide each type of benefit, together with the average size of each benefit, are presented in Table V-9.

EMPLOYER ORGANIZATIONS

In the conservative and elitist atmosphere of Colombian politics, employer groups exert considerable political influence. There are four major employer groups in Colombia, which are well established and influential, representing the coffee growers, the manufacturers, the retail merchants, and small businessmen.

TABLE V-8
Duration of Collective Agreements
(1978)

Sector	Number of Agreements: Less than 2 years	2 years	More than 2 years	Total
1. Food and Beverages	1	22	1	24
2. Metalworking	1	12	4	17
3. Textiles and Confections	3	24	0	27
4. Leather Goods	0	5	0	5
5. Chemicals	1	10	1	12
6. Printing	0	2	0	2
7. Construction	0	8	0	8
8. Lumber	0	5	0	5
9. Automotive and Automotive Parts	0	2	0	2
10. Electrical Equipment	1	3	0	4
11. Containers	0	2	0	2
12. Rubber	0	0	1	1
13. Fishing	0	2	0	2
14. Banking and Insurance	0	6	0	6
15. Other Services	0	10	0	10
16. Other Industries	1	4	1	6
Total	8	117	8	133

Source: Asociación Nacional de Industriales, "Cuadro Comparativo de Convenciones Colectivas—1978," *Convenciones Colectivas*, p. 304.

TABLE V-9
Benefits Included in Collective Bargaining Contracts (1978)

Benefit	Percentage Companies Including Benefit in Collective Contract	Average Value of Benefit
Vacation Pay	84	10-15 days' wages
Christmas Bonus	82	21-30 days' wages
Health-Care Benefits	82	Eyeglasses, annual checkup: 100% Hospitalization: worker, 60-80%; dependent, 50-70% Outpatient care: 50-70%
Death Benefits	67	1-3 months' wages
Educational Benefits		
Dependents (elementary school)	51	n.a.
Workers	44	n.a.
Sports/Recreation Benefits	41	n.a.

Source: ANDI, *Convenciones Colectivas,* pp. 308-32.
n.a. = not available.

The coffee growers are represented by the Colombian Federation of Coffee Growers (Federación de Cafeteros de Colombia—FEDECAFE). The FEDECAFE was orginally established as an informal association of coffee producers, but the importance of coffee to the national economy has gradually converted the FEDECAFE into a semi-official body: five of its eleven-member national committee are appointed by the government. The FEDECAFE buys and sells coffee and also engages in labor-related activities such as vocational training, rural education, and community organization. The FEDECAFE is one of the most prestigious organizations in Colombia, and its leaders are frequently men of national standing.

Manufacturers are represented by the ANDI. This organization was founded in 1944 and has consistently spoken out on issues of interest to business, including corporate taxation and industrial development. The ANDI promotes the study of industrial relations and offers advice on labor matters to its members, but the absence of industrywide collective bargaining in Colombia limits the importance of ANDI as a bargaining agent.

Two smaller groups, the National Federation of Merchants (Federación Nacional de Comerciantes—FENALCO) and the Colombian Association of Small Businessmen (Asociación Colombiana de la Pequeña Industria—ACOPI) are also active in representing employer interests. In recent years, several efforts have been made to coordinate the political and legislative programs of the employer groups. The economic interests of the various groups are frequently in conflict, however, and cooperation has been limited and informal.

OUTLOOK FOR ORGANIZED LABOR

Both the UTC and the CTC are sensitive to attacks from the left accusing them of being insufficiently militant in defense of workers' rights, and both major confederations contain fairly militant affiliates which are pressing for a more radical policy. Nevertheless, the UTC and the CTC are well-established and fairly traditional organizations that are not likely to adopt the type of radical policies espoused by the CSTC. Both major confederations can be expected to continue their policy of enlisting government support to accomplish their goals. Because of its historical connections to the Conservative Party, the UTC should be in a better position to do this under the Conservative administration of Belisario Betancur than under Turbay. On the other hand, the Liberal majority in the congress should enable the CTC to use its traditional influence within the Liberal Party to gain support for its policy goals. The CSTC, deeply divided on ideological issues, is not likely to become as large or as influential as the CTC and the UTC in the near future, although vigorous organizational and recruitment efforts by the two largest confederations will be required if they are to maintain their leadership role.

CHAPTER VI

Conclusion

The election of Belisario Betancur to the presidency in mid-1982 does not signify any fundamental shift in Colombia's economic or social policies. A package of economic measures enacted by the Liberal administration in February 1982 (before the elections) reduced interest rates and lowered the deposit requirement for imports in an effort to stimulate economic activity. Similar measures are to be expected from the Conservative regime headed by Betancur, perhaps with greater emphasis on improving productivity in the agricultural sector. The generally favorable attitude toward foreign investment is not likely to change under Betancur.

Betancur's campaign statements concerning amnesty for suspected terrorists and reconciliation with the various revolutionary groups that exist in the country are similar to statements made during other presidential campaigns. The basic obstacle to such a reconciliation is that the revolutionary groups reject elections as a means of determining the composition of the government. These groups aim at a restructuring of Colombian society, which the major political parties and the vast majority of Colombians do not accept. Sporadic guerilla activity is therefore likely to continue in the foreseeable future, without having any major effect on the stability of the government.

The Colombian economy entered the 1980s in sound condition, particularly in comparison to most Latin American economies. The foreign currency reserve position continued to be solid through the first quarter of 1982; gross reserves on March 31, 1982, were US$5.3 billion, or considerably more than a full year's worth of imports.[1] The two major sources of Colombia's export boom in the late 1970s (increased coffee sales and increased sales of illegal drugs) have reached plateaus and will probably not in-

[1] "Colombia," *Bank of London and South America Review*, Vol. 16, No. II/82, p. 97.

crease very rapidly in the 1980s, but the prospect of large new exports of coal and other minerals could replace coffee and illegal drugs as a stimulus for the external sector of the economy. Preliminary projections indicate that net income (to Colombia) from the Cerrejón coal project alone could be US$1.2 billion per year by 1990.[2] Apart from direct income from coal, the existence of large coal fields and natural gas deposits in the northern part of the country should promote considerable industrial investment in that region. In the longer term, there are strong possibilities for growth in the synthetic fuels industry because of the large energy surplus in this area of the country.

On the domestic economic front, the principal problems are low capital investment and outdated industrial facilities. Like other developing countries which shielded their young industries from foreign competition for many years, Colombia is now facing the necessity to compete on an international level for manufactured exports and to rationalize its domestic industry in order to meet the challenge of imported technology in a relatively unprotected environment. The usual conflict between economic logic (which suggests that Colombia should concentrate on those industries in which it has a competitive advantage) and social pressures (which demand the protection of jobs in noncompetitive industries) may intensify in the 1980s as high interest rates continue to dampen domestic investment in productivity improvement. A continuing expansion of the economy would probably keep the conflict between the two objectives (competitiveness and job protection) under control, but unexpected economic shocks could increase the pressure for protectionist policies.

Colombia's political stability and steady economic growth have enabled it to achieve and maintain a good international credit standing. Investment of private foreign capital is also substantial and should continue to increase. Shifts in economic policy during the 1970s and early 1980s were generally gradual, enabling foreign companies to plan ahead and adapt to the new conditions. Finally, Colombia weathered the storm of violence of the 1950s and emerged with a stable democracy which, despite its defects, should continue to allow for steady economic growth and improvement of social conditions.

---

[2] "The rich promise of north coast coal deposits," *Financial Times*, February 19, 1982, p. 29.

APPENDIXES

Appendix A

FIGURE A-1

Population Structure by Sex and Age Group
(actual 1975 and projected 2000)

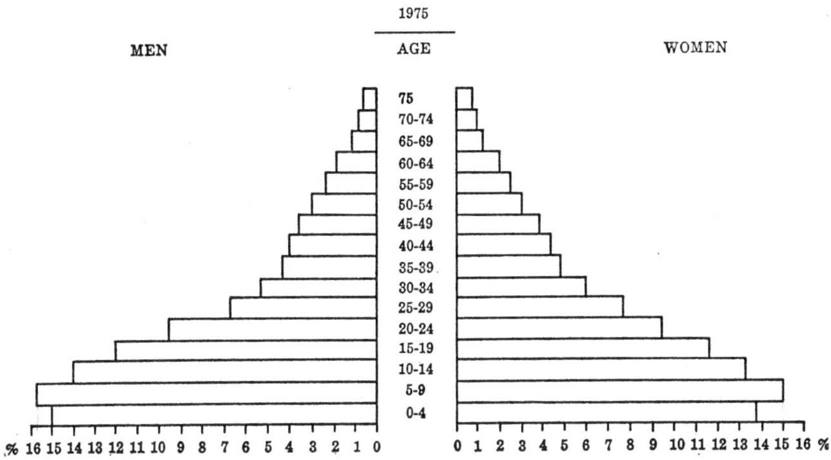

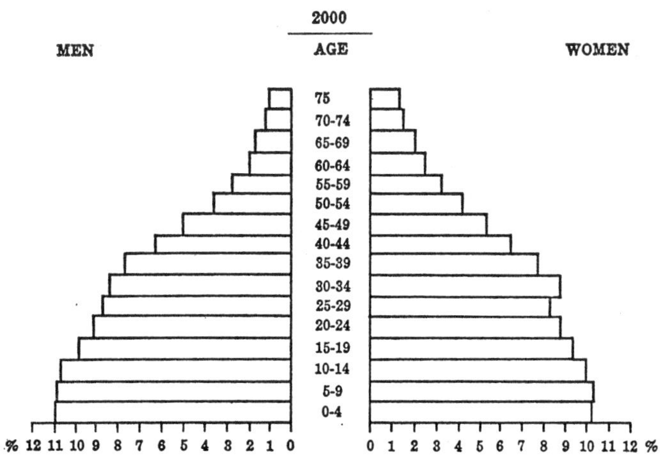

Source: DNP, *Plan de Integración Nacional,* Vol. II, p. 50.

Appendix B

TABLE B-1
Forecasted Economically Active Population in 1985 and 1990—High Alternative[a]
(thousands)

	Men			
	1985		1990	
Age Group	Urban	Rural	Urban	Rural
10-14	65.9	78.1	78.6	75.3
15-19	493.7	396.8	526.3	349.4
20-24	1,051.4	486.0	1,094.4	426.9
25-34	1,651.9	696.2	2,191.1	780.0
35-44	973.8	407.1	1,290.7	455.8
45-54	680.9	286.4	785.1	278.8
55-64	401.8	180.5	490.5	186.0
64	139.2	91.1	166.4	92.0
Total	5,458.6	2,622.2	6,623.1	2,644.2

	Women			
	1985		1990	
Age Group	Urban	Rural	Urban	Rural
10-14	63.6	14.2	65.3	13.1
15-19	432.4	63.8	562.2	69.6
20-24	476.7	64.5	496.1	55.3
25-34	616.5	99.9	757.6	101.3
35-44	361.8	65.3	495.7	71.6
45-54	245.4	53.7	289.7	52.6
55-64	99.8	34.0	124.9	35.5
64	26.4	15.3	31.9	16.7
Total	2,322.6	410.7	2,823.4	415.7

TABLE B-1 (continued)

Age Group	Both Sexes					
	1985			1990		
	Urban	Rural	Total	Urban	Rural	Total
10-14	129.5	92.3	221.8	143.9	88.4	232.3
15-19	926.1	460.6	1,386.7	1,088.5	419.0	1,507.5
20-24	1,528.1	550.5	2,078.6	1,590.5	482.2	2,072.7
25-34	2,268.4	796.1	3,064.5	2,948.7	881.3	3,830.0
35-44	1,335.6	472.4	1,808.0	1,786.4	527.4	2,313.8
45-54	926.3	340.1	1,266.4	1,074.8	331.4	1,406.2
55-64	501.6	214.5	716.1	615.4	221.5	836.9
64	165.6	106.4	272.0	198.3	108.7	307.0
Total	7,781.2	3,032.9	10,814.1	9,446.5	3,059.9	12,506.4

Source: Hernando Gómez Buendía, "Perspectivas Ocupacionales," *La Economía Colombiana en la década de los Ochenta*, p. 83.

[a] High Alternative—based on increases in life expectancy at birth of 0.5 years per calendar year, together with a decline in fertility rate from 4.2 children per woman to 3.9 children per woman between 1976 and 1988.

TABLE B-2

Forecasted Economically Active Population in 1985 and 1990—Low Alternative [a]

(thousands)

	Men			
	1985		1990	
Age Group	Urban	Rural	Urban	Rural
10-14	63.0	69.5	61.9	57.1
15-19	493.7	396.8	545.0	361.4
20-24	1,051.4	486.0	1,094.4	426.9
25-34	1,651.9	696.2	2,191.1	780.0
35-44	973.8	407.1	1,290.7	455.8
45-54	680.9	286.4	785.1	278.8
55-64	401.8	180.5	400.5	186.0
64	131.1	87.6	151.0	90.1
Total	5,447.6	2,610.1	6,609.7	2,636.1

	Women			
	1985		1990	
Age Group	Urban	Rural	Urban	Rural
10-14	53.2	11.1	59.4	10.7
15-19	415.5	61.3	462.4	57.2
20-24	476.7	64.5	496.1	55.3
25-34	616.5	99.9	757.6	101.3
35-44	361.8	61.3	495.7	71.6
45-54	245.4	53.7	289.7	52.6
55-64	99.8	34.0	124.9	35.5
64	24.4	16.6	30.8	13.0
Total	2,293.3	402.4	2,716.6	397.2

TABLE B-2 (continued)

	Both Sexes					
	1985			1990		
Age Group	Urban	Rural	Total	Urban	Rural	Total
10-14	116.2	80.6	196.8	121.3	67.8	189.1
15-19	909.2	458.1	1,367.3	1,007.4	418.6	1,426.0
20-24	1,528.1	550.5	2,078.6	1,590.5	482.2	2,072.3
25-34	2,268.4	796.1	3,064.5	2,948.7	881.3	3,830.0
35-44	1,335.6	472.4	1,808.0	1,786.4	527.4	2,313.8
45-54	926.4	340.1	1,266.4	1,074.8	331.3	1,406.2
55-64	501.6	214.5	716.1	615.4	221.5	836.9
64	155.5	100.2	255.7	181.8	103.1	284.9
Total	7,740.9	3,012.5	10,753.4	9,326.3	3,033.3	12,359.7

Source: Hernando Gómez Buendía, "Perspectivas Ocupacionales," *La Economía Colombiana en la Década de los Ochenta,* p. 84.

[a] Low Alternative—based on increases in life expectancy at birth of 0.5 years per calendar year, together with a decline in fertility from 4.2 children per woman in 1976 to 2.5 children per woman in 1988.

Index

Racial Policies of American Industry Series

1. *The Negro in the Automobile Industry*, by Herbert R. Northrup. 1968
2. *The Negro in the Aerospace Industry*, by Herbert R. Northrup. 1968
3. *The Negro in the Steel Industry*, by Richard L. Rowan. 1968
4. *The Negro in the Hotel Industry*, by Edward C. Koziara and Karen S. Koziara. 1968
5. *The Negro in the Petroleum Industry*, by Carl B. King and Howard W. Risher, Jr. 1969
6. *The Negro in the Rubber Tire Industry*, by Herbert R. Northrup and Alan B. Batchelder. 1969
7. *The Negro in the Chemical Industry*, by William Howard Quay, Jr. 1969
8. *The Negro in the Paper Industry*, by Herbert R. Northrup. 1969
9. *The Negro in the Banking Industry*, by Armand J. Thieblot, Jr. 1970
10. *The Negro in the Public Utility Industries*, by Bernard E. Anderson. 1970
11. *The Negro in the Insurance Industry*, by Linda P. Fletcher. 1970
12. *The Negro in the Meat Industry*, by Walter A. Fogel. 1970
13. *The Negro in the Tobacco Industry*, by Herbert R. Northrup. 1970
14. *The Negro in the Bituminous Coal Mining Industry*, by Darold T. Barnum. 1970
15. *The Negro in the Trucking Industry*, by Richard D. Leone. 1970
16. *The Negro in the Railroad Industry*, by Howard W. Risher, Jr. 1971
17. *The Negro in the Shipbuilding Industry*, by Lester Rubin. 1970
18. *The Negro in the Urban Transit Industry*, by Philip W. Jeffress. 1970
19. *The Negro in the Lumber Industry*, by John C. Howard. 1970
20. *The Negro in the Textile Industry*, by Richard L. Rowan. 1970
21. *The Negro in the Drug Manufacturing Industry*, by F. Marion Fletcher. 1970
22. *The Negro in the Department Store Industry*, by Charles R. Perry. 1971
23. *The Negro in the Air Transport Industry*, by Herbert R. Northrup et al. 1971
24. *The Negro in the Drugstore Industry*, by F. Marion Fletcher. 1971
25. *The Negro in the Supermarket Industry*, by Gordon F. Bloom and F. Marion Fletcher. 1972
26. *The Negro in the Farm Equipment and Construction Machinery Industry*, by Robert Ozanne. 1972
27. *The Negro in the Electrical Manufacturing Industry*, by Theodore V. Purcell and Daniel P. Mulvey. 1971
28. *The Negro in the Furniture Industry*, by William E. Fulmer. 1973
29. *The Negro in the Longshore Industry*, by Lester Rubin and William S. Swift. 1974
30. *The Negro in the Offshore Maritime Industry*, by William S. Swift. 1974
31. *The Negro in the Apparel Industry*, by Elaine Gale Wrong. 1974

STUDIES OF NEGRO EMPLOYMENT

Vol. I. *Negro Employment in Basic Industry: A Study of Racial Policies in Six Industries (Automobile, Aerospace, Steel, Rubber Tires, Petroleum, and Chemicals)*, by Herbert R. Northrup, Richard L. Rowan, et al. 1970. *

Vol. II. *Negro Employment in Finances: A Study of Racial Policies in Banking and Insurance*, by Armand J. Thieblot, Jr., and Linda Pickthorne Fletcher. 1970. *

Vol. III. *Negro Employment in Public Utilities: A Study of Racial Policies in the Electric Power, Gas, and Telephone Industries*, by Bernard E. Anderson. 1970. *

Vol. IV. *Negro Employment in Southern Industry: A Study of Racial Policies in the Paper, Lumber, Tobacco, Coal Mining, and Textile Industries*, by Herbert R. Northrup, Richard L. Rowan, et al. 1971. *

Vol. V. *Negro Employment in Land and Air Transport: A Study of Racial Policies in the Railroad, Airline, Trucking, and Urban Transit Industries*, by Herbert R. Northrup, Howard W. Risher, Jr., Richard D. Leone, and Philip W. Jeffress. 1971. $13.50

Vol. VI. *Negro Employment in Retail Trade: A Study of Racial Policies in the Department Store, Drugstore, and Supermarket Industries*, by Gordon F. Bloom, F. Marion Fletcher, and Charles R. Perry. 1972. *

Vol. VII. *Negro Employment in the Maritime Industries: A Study of Racial Policies in the Shipbuilding, Longshore, and Offshore Maritime Industries*, by Lester Rubin, William S. Swift, and Herbert R. Northrup. 1974. *

Vol. VIII. *Black and Other Minority Participation in the All-Volunteer Navy and Marine Corps*, by Herbert R. Northrup, Steven M. DiAntonio, John A. Brinker, and Dale F. Daniel. 1979. *

Order from the Industrial Research Unit
The Wharton School, University of Pennsylvania
Philadelphia, Pennsylvania 19104

* Order these books from University Microfilms, Inc., Attn: Books Editorial Department, 300 North Zeeb Road, Ann Arbor, Michigan 48106.